The Unsolved Mysteries
Of Star Wars
By Stuart Carapola

I dedicate this book to my daughter Emelia, who not only latched onto Star Wars with all the enthusiasm of her old man at a very young age, but practically demanded a Darth Vader party for her third birthday. You make this old Jedi proud!

Table of Contents

Bonus Features

Introduction

I think it's safe to say that Star Wars is a cultural phenomenon like no other. The tale of the Skywalker family, the Jedi and Sith Orders, and the mysterious and powerful Force have both tantalized generations of fans and made George Lucas a ton of money.

Interest in the franchise has renewed with the imminent release of the third, and final, trilogy in the Star Wars saga, completing a story that will have spanned an almost forty year telling. This makes Star Wars one of the longest-running movie franchises of all time, but those long years between trilogies are also what made this book possible.

Through either lack of foresight, a conscious decision to prioritize central storylines over inconsequential minutae, or just general lazy writing, the Star Wars movies are LOADED with inconsistencies and plot points that were teased and then never touched on again. With a fanbase as large as Star Wars, it's inevitable that these inconsistencies take on a life of their own and form the basis for long-running fan theories.

As viewers, we realize that we're probably not supposed to spend too much time thinking about these things, but when you're dealing with movies whose stories are often referred to as mythologies, it's only natural that diehard fans are going to want to dive in a little deeper and work out answers to the plot holes. These are the things that casual fans will probably never even notice, but people like me do, and in my case, I decided to make a book out of it.

With that in mind, I hope you enjoy this look at...THE UNSOLVED MYSTERIES OF STAR WARS!

Did Darth Vader Realize Palpatine Lied About Padme's Death When He Discovered Luke?

The last time Anakin Skywalker saw his wife Padme alive was on the planet Mustafar at the end of Revenge Of The Sith. Anakin attacked her with the Force choke, causing her to collapse and setting up his fateful battle against Obi-Wan Kenobi. Obi-Wan carried Padme back into their ship after defeating his former pupil, and they flew off to safety while Anakin (or what was left of him) was abandoned to die on Mustafar.

While Emperor Palpatine did eventually show up and rescue Anakin by reconstructing him into Darth Vader, Palpatine informed Vader that, in his anger, he had killed Padme. Though Padme did indeed die shortly after the events of Mustafar, she did live long enough to give birth to Luke and Leia before giving up the ghost.

Fast forward twenty years: while dealing with the threat of a growing rebellion, Darth Vader discovers a Force-sensitive young man named Luke Skywalker in their midst, fighting alongside his former mentor Obi Wan. As the crawler at the beginning of Empire Strikes Back said, Vader became obsessed with tracking Luke down, finally confronting him at Cloud City and revealing the true nature of their relationship.

Strangely, despite what had to be a completely unexpected discovery by Vader in light of what Palpatine had told him about Padme's fate, Vader seems surprisingly calm about the revelation that she had apparently survived long enough to bear his child. Did it ever occur to him that Palpatine had lied, or was that even a consideration given his obsession with finding Luke?

We actually have two questions to answer here: obviously there's the issue of Vader's reaction to his discovery, but we also need to establish whether or not Palpatine even knew for sure whether Padme had survived the encounter on Mustafar. Palpatine himself hadn't seen Padme or Obi-Wan depart Mustafar, so there wouldn't appear to be any obvious way he would know whether she had lived or died.

However, as he has demonstrated many times throughout the movies, Palpatine's affinity with the Dark Side has given him insight into events he shouldn't have knowledge of, and in many cases even events that haven't happened yet. His battle with Yoda also showed him to be every bit as strong with the Force as the Jedi Master, so if Yoda can sense the deaths of of Jedi spread throughout the galaxy during the Jedi Purge, it stands to reason that Palpatine should detect the birth of not one, but two children who are supposedly at least as strong with the Force as Anakin.

Then again, Vader's brief conversation with his master in the Empire Strikes Back would seem to indicate that Palpatine was as surprised by Luke's existence as Vader was. This could be because...

Palpatine really had no idea that Padme had survived long enough to give birth to Luke and Leia.

This is possible, but seems the least likely. While Vader might have been fooled by the way Padme was made up to look like she was still pregnant at her funeral (if he was even aware the funeral happened), it's hard to believe that the all-knowing Palpatine didn't at least have some idea that Anakin's children had survived.

Having watched every step Palpatine took to manipulate events toward his ultimate goal of supreme power over the galaxy, you can see that he was not prone to leaving things to chance. If he told Vader that Padme was dead, you could bet that he would follow up and make 100% sure that she and her unborn child (children) were definitely dead so that they wouldn't suddenly pop up at some point down the line and make him look like a liar.

That is, unless he didn't think it would matter because....

Palpatine knew Luke and Leia were born, but didn't consider them a threat until the destruction of the first Death Star.

Again, not likely since Palpatine would have probably sensed their strength with the Force from day one, but perhaps Palpatine assumed that even if Anakin's children survived, they would be relegated to their respective upbringings (Luke as a subsistence farmer on Tatooine, Leia as the daughter of a Senator) and would never become a threat to him. Even if he knew of their strength with the Force, he may have assumed that with the Jedi wiped out (except for Obi-Wan and possibly Yoda), they would never receive the guidance they would need to become a threat.

Once Luke caught his attention by firing the shot that destroyed the Death Star, especially with Vader on his tail, Palpatine reconsidered his assessment. He decided that Luke at least was powerful enough to be reckoned with, and sent Vader to try and turn him to the Dark Side.

Palpatine knew Luke and Leia were born, and intentionally withheld their existence from Vader for his own purposes.

Loyalty was never one of Palpatine's best qualities, and it's possible that he knew full well that Luke and Leia had survived and would grow up to be every bit as strong with the Force as their father. The same way Palpatine had knowingly set Count Dooku up to be killed by Anakin, perhaps Palpatine may have been planning the same for Vader, waiting until his children

4

grew up and were powerful enough that one or both of them would slay their father and take his place as Palpatine's new apprentice.

This would seem to have at least been Palpatine's plan at the end, as he spent the last moments of his life trying to convince Luke to kill Vader and become his new apprentice. It fit with Palpatine's history, as he had manipulated Anakin into his service almost the exact same way. The difference was that, unlike Anakin, Luke would walk away in one piece and not subject to the restrictions Vader's injuries had imposed on him.

Palpatine had always planned for Anakin to become his unstoppable enforcer once he grew to adulthood and learned to harness his power. When his once-promising apprentice was maimed at the hands of Obi-Wan and reconstructed in a much more physically limited form, it may be that Palpatine immediately made the decision to wait until Luke and Leia came of age so he could manipulate them into becoming the powerful servant(s) he had planned Vader to be.

After looking at the different possible scenarios, it's hard to believe that Palpatine didn't have at least had some idea that it wasn't as simple as "Padme's dead, end of story." But with that in mind, let's look at how Vader might have reacted to discovering his son alive and running around on the Death Star twenty years later. Vader never confronted Palpatine about it, but he had to have spent a good deal of time rolling everything around in his head and trying to figure out how this was possible.

While Vader never spoke about whatever conclusions he may have come to, they probably boiled down to the following:

Vader assumed Palpatine didn't know any more than he did, and instead blamed Obi-Wan.

While his master was obviously nobody's fool,

Anakin/Vader appears to be a complete sucker for whatever the Emperor told him. Despite Palpatine's clearly shady character and the fact that, for all intents and purposes, he forced Anakin to swear loyalty to him in exchange for saving Padme (which never happened, by the way), Vader never seemed to have a second thought about remaining by the Emperor's side even after his choice to become a Sith apprentice cost him everything.

Vader surely was witness to many, many more instances of Palpatine's duplicitous tactics in the years after the Fall of the Jedi and, by the time he discovered Luke, there's no way he could have had any illusions about who he was serving. In spite of all that, we got the scene in Empire Strikes Back where Vader actually works out a plan with his master to subvert his son rather than question the fact that he was there at all.

It stands to reason that Vader blamed Obi-Wan for hiding Luke from him. In fact, it would make sense that Vader blamed Obi-Wan for everything that had happened to him: Padme's death, his own physical destruction, and the eventual discovery that Luke survived and had been hidden from him. Remember, twenty years had passed since his battle with Obi-Wan on Mustafar, and that is a LOT of time to let a grudge simmer.

Defeating Obi-Wan on the Death Star was a moment he had been looking forward to for a very long time, yet Vader apparently continued to carry around a need to beat his former master even after their final battle. The fact that he actually said that "Obi-Wan's failure is now complete" upon discovering that Luke had a twin sister seems to bear that out. Vader held Obi War responsible for everything, and it may just have never occurred to him that Palpatine had misled him.

Vader had spent enough time with Palpatine by this point to know how he operates, and wasn't surprised to find out he had been deceived.

6

Vader as we touched on a moment ago, had to have become very familiar with Emperor Palpatine's deceptive ways after spending twenty years by his side. While Vader may have been surprised to discover Luke was alive, he may not have been as surprised to find out he had been lied to as we would think.

In fact, if you look back at the history of the Sith, the entire lineage is loaded with examples of Sith Masters and apprentices continually trying to outmaneuver one another in a cutthroat struggle for dominance. As strange as it seems, it could be that he knew Palpatine lied, but just didn't care that much.

Vader realized that Palpatine had lied to him, and began plotting to usurp him.

If Vader suddenly grew a brain and looked at the facts staring him in the face, he would realize that Padme didn't die on Mustafar after all, and that Palpatine had lied about how his rage had killed her. Once Vader began putting the pieces together and came to grips with the fact that Palpatine deceived him, he may have decided to follow the long-standing Sith tradition and kill his master for his treachery.

If Vader did make a move on Palpatine, the goal would have likely included not just taking over the Empire, but also becoming the new Sith Master with Luke as his apprentice. Vader asking Luke to join him in overthrowing the Emperor and ruling the galaxy as father and son lends credence to this theory.

Don't forget, the idea of usurping Palpatine had begun rolling around in Vader's head long before he discovered Luke, and he said as much not long after swearing his loyalty to Palpatine in the first place. Right before the battle with Obi-Wan on Mustafar, Anakin gave Padme pretty much the exact same speech he would give Luke years later, telling her that he could kill Palpatine so they could rule the galaxy together. Anakin's lust for power was even visible as far back as the incident when

7

he returned to Tatooine just in time to witness his mother's death. After wiping out the sand people, Anakin lashed out with a tirade about how he should be all powerful, and one day would be.

The first step of Vader's plan would be to convince the Emperor that Luke would make a powerful ally if he could be turned, and not to kill him as the Emperor originally wanted. Vader was only partially truthful, because while he would indeed see that potential in Luke, it would be as his own ally, not the Emperor's.

Even if Vader wanted ultimate power, he may have been held back from making a move if he wasn't sure he could take Palpatine by himself. At the very least, the possibility that Palpatine's Sith lightning could destroy his life support suit (which it eventually did) would be enough to stay Vader's hand.

Luke, however, did not have the same limitation. Perhaps using Luke as a surrogate, or at least letting Luke do the heavy lifting while Vader supported him from a distance with the Force, an alliance with his son would provide Vader with the opportunity he had been waiting for all this time.

Did Palpatine Intentionally Lose The Fight Against Mace Windu?

In Episode III, Chancellor Palpatine is finally revealed as the Sith Lord the Jedi had spent the better part of twenty years searching for. Mace Windu takes a team of Jedi to arrest him and, wanting to avoid any complications resulting from Anakin Skywalker's long-standing relationship with Palpatine, gives Anakin strict instructions to stay behind. Anakin is unhappy, but grudgingly complies...until he changes his mind and follows Windu to Palpatine's chambers.

After a hard fought battle that saw Palpatine easily take out Windu's entire team within seconds, Windu has Palpatine at his mercy when Anakin, in violation of Windu's orders, arrives and tries to convince Windu not to kill Palpatine. Windu, feeling that Palpatine is too dangerous to let live, prepares to strike Palpatine down when Anakin intervenes, cutting Windu's lightsaber hand off and allowing Palpatine to dispose of Windu once and for all with his Sith lightning.

Anakin's interference in the Windu-Palpatine confrontation couldn't have been more timely...leading one to wonder if Palpatine could have killed Windu all along and intentionally threw the fight, knowing it would lead to the outcome we saw with Anakin becoming his new Sith apprentice. Was Palpatine a good enough puppetmaster that he could foresee that exact result, or was he really on the ropes until Anakin showed up just in the nick of time?

Let's break this down into the two key points we have to answer:

Could Palpatine have been 100% certain that Anakin would show up to save him?

The first thing to point out is that intentionally not bringing your best to a fight with Mace Windu would be a BIG risk for anyone to take, even Palpatine. A certainty, or at least a very strong belief, that things would play out as they did would be necessary for this to be something he would even consider.

It's entirely possible that this is the case since Palpatine was not known for making rash decisions. The entire prequel trilogy illustrated the skill with which Palpatine planned out every minor detail in advance and took as much time as necessary to let everything play out as desired:

-He instigated the Trade Federation's blockade on Naboo for the sole purpose of creating the crisis he'd need to manipulate Padme into calling for a vote of no confidence in Chancellor Vallorum. This set the stage for his own election to that post thanks to the sympathy vote the invasion elicited.

-After letting the galactic civil war go on for a full decade, he saw an opportunity to take advantage of the simple Jar Jar Binks when he covered for Padme as a substitute Senator during her retreat to Naboo. Palpatine talked Jar Jar into motioning for him to be granted emergency war powers, giving Palpatine a blank check to act as he saw fit with no accountability.

-He spent almost Anakin's entire life sowing the seeds that caused him to doubt the Jedi's true intentions, then when the time was right, tempted him with a solution to his fear of losing Padme. The preparation time was well spent because Anakin did the unthinkable and chose Palpatine over Mace Windu when the chips were down.

Given that he was patient enough to take the twenty years or so that it took for his plan to play out, I doubt that Palpatine suddenly got reckless at the end and picked a fight he wasn't sure he'd win. He knew Anakin would come, otherwise there's no way he would have picked a fight with such a powerful, senior member of the Jedi Council.

Was Palpatine strong enough that he could have beaten Mace Windu if he wanted?

All signs point to yes. For one, he took out Windu's entire team as soon as the fight started, quickly turning it into a much more manageable one-on-one fight. Windu was no dummy, and for a fight like this, he wouldn't have just grabbed the first three Jedi he saw. He would have chosen the three toughest warriors he had available, and if Palpatine was able to cut through them that easily, it doesn't seem like a stretch to say that he could have probably taken Windu as well.

Also, Palpatine seems to be a stronger practitioner of the Force than anyone else in the Star Wars saga. While I normally try to avoid "he used the Force" to explain away things I can't come up with a rational explanation for, he did show himself to be powerful enough to make Yoda run for his life when they fought later on.

While not known for being the elite warrior Windu was, Yoda was clearly recognized as the Jedi's highest authority on use of the Force for everything from feeling mass killings from light years away to stopping massive boulders from crushing his friends. Despite that, Yoda couldn't get close enough to Palpatine to do any damage because Palpatine was using the Force to literally rip the Senate chamber apart and throw pieces of it at the Jedi Master before running him off completely with his Sith lightning.

Palpatine was able to hang with Windu long enough that it seems like he was never in any serious trouble, and was strong enough to defeat Windu if it came down to it. He knew that Anakin's initial reaction to his revelation of being a Sith Lord would have led to the confrontation we saw, but was also certain that Anakin wouldn't let his only hope of saving Padme be

11

destroyed. Palpatine knew exactly how everything would play out, and decided that the time was right to pull the trigger and set the final wheels on his plan into motion.

When Yoda Said "No, There Is Another," Are We Sure He Meant Leia?

When Luke Skywalker decided to end his training early to go save his friends on Bespin in spite of his promise to Yoda that he would finish what he started, Yoda and Obi Wan were understandably unhappy. Now with the benefit of the hindsight that Episode III provided us with, it's clear how wary they were of history repeating itself if Luke turned to the Dark Side the way Anakin had.

Despite their warnings of the danger he was putting himself in by facing Vader before he was ready, Luke's mind was set and, as his father had done many times in his own youth, he ignored the advice of Yoda and Obi Wan and followed his heart instead. Obi Wan lamented how Luke was their last hope as his ship took off, but in the light of the X-Wing's thrusters, Yoda simply stated "No...there is another."

As we came to discover in Return of the Jedi, Leia turned out to be Luke's twin sister, and though she never had to interject herself into the situation involving Luke, Vader, and Emperor Palpatine, the clear implication was that she would be the true last hope if Luke failed to destroy the Sith. But are we sure about that?

Given that Leia never actually had to face the Sith herself, we never found out what kind of power she truly possessed, or even that she possessed any to begin with. Is it possible that we've been mistaken for all these years, and that Leia wasn't the "other" of whom Yoda spoke?

Before considering other possible candidates, let's first analyze Leia's contributions in the original trilogy, and see what exactly she brought to the table as a member of the Rebellion:

A New Hope: Leia manages to record the message to Obi Wan and sends C-3PO and R2-D2 on their way, but almost immediately gets shot and taken captive on the Death Star. She's rescued by Han and Luke, who look past her snarky attitude long enough to fight their way out of the Death Star with Leia bringing up the rear while they did all the work.

They escape and head to the rebel base on Yavin, and Leia stands there looking concerned while Luke and Han fight their way past the Imperial fighters and destroy the Death Star. She closes the movie with a display of truly excellent leadership by awarding medals to Luke and Han while completely ignoring Chewbacca, who risked his life every bit as much as Han and Luke did.

The Empire Strikes Back: Leia spends the entire first part of the movie on Hoth sulking and complaining while Luke nearly dies several times over and Han risks his life to go out and search for him instead of leaving to settle matters with Jabba the Hutt. From there, she spends the next bit complaining because Han can't get the hyperdrive working, then she gets scared by the Mynocks on the windshield in the asteroid and makes Han and Chewie go out and fight them off.

After that, they're off to Cloud City where she complains about Lando and questions Han's judgment in bringing her to the one place he thought they MIGHT be safe, as if there was a Starbucks or somewhere they could go instead. She does nothing while Han is tortured and interrogated, and then finally, as he's about to be frozen in Carbonite, she breaks down and admits she loves Han, who seems unwilling to return the sentiment for some reason.

Next, she has Lando (you know, the guy she didn't trust) rescue her from Cloud City, then gets Chewie to threaten to kill him if he doesn't turn back to get Luke. The movie closes with her standing around in the spaceship equivalent of a log cabin living room with a roaring fire and hot chocolate while Lando and

Chewie prepare to go about the extremely dangerous task of rescuing Han from Jabba.

Return Of The Jedi: Leia comes up with a good enough disguise to get into Jabba's Palace, but gets caught almost immediately and is forced to wear the infamous golden bikini for Jabba's amusement. Luke shows up to rescue everyone and, in the ensuing confusion, Leia chokes Jabba to death with her chain.

That is literally the first useful thing she did in the entire trilogy, albeit it was done to a villain who wasn't exactly nimble enough to get away from her. Meanwhile, Luke, Han, Lando, and Chewie did all the real work by wiping out the other 57 members of Jabba's gang and rescuing the droids from the sand they had fallen into.

So everyone heads to the forest moon of Endor where, due to her substandard driving skills, she gets knocked out and surrounded by Imperial troopers. She was rescued by a midget bear, who then takes her hostage himself and brings her back to his tree village where they give her a dress and braid her hair. She is no help whatsoever when her friends get captured by the Ewoks, and C-3PO had to defy his programming and impersonate a god to stop the Ewoks from sacrificing them.

After that, she finds out Luke is her twin brother, and wastes no time telling him to run away before they all get caught if Vader is able to track him down. The fact that Luke is her brother means that Vader is also her father, but that doesn't really seem to register with her for some reason. She is fearful for Luke's safety, but stays in character by blowing Han off when he tries to comfort her.

She gets shot during the assault on the shield generator, but she pulls off Useful Act #2 and shoots a trooper who was getting ready to capture she and Han. Sure, it was one trooper out of a few hundred, and Chewie would have bailed them out with the Imperial Walker in another ten seconds anyway, but it counts. She does nothing else for the rest of the movie other than tell Han that Luke is her brother, and then dance with her savage captors after everyone else defeated the Empire for her.

Now that we've recapped nearly her every move, it's kind of a struggle to see how this war couldn't have been won without her. In fact, the Empire would have probably been destroyed halfway through the first movie if she wasn't there to slow the others down.

We may see Leia demonstrate actual power in the new trilogy, but she has never shown any evidence of an affinity with the Force so far, and Yoda and Obi Wan would have been nuts to expect anything out of her even if she did given the way she conducted herself during the Rebellion. But if not her, then who else could Yoda have been speaking of?

Folks, just watch Return of the Jedi again, because the answer was in front of your face the whole time. Anyone else notice that Luke actually didn't destroy Vader or Palpatine? Remember who did? That's right…Darth Vader! What if, even after Anakin turned to the Dark Side and wiped out the Jedi, there was some part of Yoda that thought he still could come through and fulfill the prophecy

Well, he technically already did that at the end of Episode III when there were two Sith (Palpatine and Vader) and two surviving Jedi (Obi-Wan and Yoda) left standing. It's possible that the Jedi may have misunderstood the prophecy to mean that Anakin would destroy the Sith when his role could have been to merely even up the numbers. But for the sake of this discussion, we'll overlook that possibility for now and go with the Jedi definition instead.

This theory might seem crazy, but most people who think that Yoda was talking about Leia probably grew up on the original trilogy and have the perspective that Star Wars is a story about Luke Skywalker emerging from a humble life in the middle of nowhere, coming of age, accepting the responsibility his father cast aside, and bringing peace to the galaxy. All those things about Luke are true, but if you follow the six episodes in order from beginning to end, you realize that's only part of the bigger picture.

Star Wars is actually a story about Anakin Skywalker practically being raised to become the Chosen One, losing everyone who ever mattered to him, and eventually letting his frustrations and anger destroy him and turn him into Darth Vader. He would remain in that state for decades before the son he never knew he had suddenly appeared and dragged out the inner good he thought was gone long ago. Finally, when it all came to pass and he had to make the choice, he cast Palpatine into the shaft, saved Luke, destroyed the Sith for good, and redeemed himself in the process.

Now, it could just be that Yoda really did mean Leia for some reason and he was as surprised as anyone when things played out as they did with Anakin, but if that was the case, then why would Obi-Wan assume that Luke was the last hope? Putting blatant sexism aside as a possibility for a moment, he was right there when Leia was born, and he had to know exactly who she was when he got the message from her via R2-D2. Could it be that he didn't sense any strength with the Force in Leia, but did in Luke?

In spite of everything we've assumed for 30 years, there's nothing to suggest that Leia had any use of the Force, or that she had the emotional stability or maturity to confront the Sith even if she did. The fact that Obi-Wan thought Luke was their only hope would suggest that he agreed, and even if he and Yoda had given up on Anakin long ago, both Luke and Padme turned out to be right when they sensed the good in him that eventually led to the Fall of the Sith.

Was Palpatine Aware of Anakin's Existence Before The Events Of The Phantom Menace?

When Qui Gon Jinn was forced to touch down on Tatooine to repair the ship he and the fugitive Queen Amidala had escaped Naboo in, he was astonished to discover a young slave boy who had apparently been conceived by the Force. Anakin Skywalker had a higher mitichlorian count than even Yoda, and Qui Gonn quickly came to the conclusion that Anakin had to be the Chosen One who would bring balance to the Force.

While Anakin was initially refused entry to the Jedi Order on the basis of being too old to begin training, he continued to accompany Qui Gon and Obi Wan Kenobi as they returned to Naboo to aid in the battle against the Trade Federation. While Qui Gon was killed by Darth Maul, Anakin piloted a ship up to the Trade Federation mother ship, destroying it and bringing the Federation troops to their knees.

Upon his return to Naboo, Anakin was informed that Obi Wan had been promoted to the rank of Jedi Knight and would be allowed to take him on as his Padawan apprentice. In a chilling foreshadowing, Chancellor Palpatine, who was actually the powerful Sith Lord Darth Sidious, gave Anakin a pat on the shoulder and made a passing remark about watching his career with great interest.

The discovery of such a pivotal figure as Anakin in such an unlikely place seemed to be an entirely chance-driven event, but was is truly? Is it possible that Palpatine not only planned to subvert Anakin to the Sith cause after he was brought to Coruscant, but was aware of him before even the Jedi? Palpatine had used the Force to gain incredible foresight into events to come, but could he have known that Anakin would get pulled into the conflict and become available for his uses?

Let's go through all the possibilities raised by this series of events and see what we can piece together:

Palpatine knew about Anakin, and planned to subvert him from the beginning.

Palpatine approached his rise to power like a decades-long chess game, and he was not at all adverse to sacrificing a pawn or two if it moved him closer to his goals. He sacrificed Darth Maul to draw the Jedi out and put a scare in them by letting them know that the Sith were still there and a threat to them. He then sacrificed Count Dooku to push Anakin further toward the selfish mindset he exploited to eventually gain his subservience and transform him into Darth Vader. In fact, Palpatine was ready to sacrifice Vader as well once Luke bested him on the Death Star.

This history shows that Palpatine regarded others as little more than tools to use to his own ends. If he had detected Anakin and his affinity with the Force, it would be very much in character if he merely saw Anakin as another such tool that he could use when the time was right. The only part that would have surprised Palpatine would be that the Jedi got to Anakin before he did.

Palpatine had no idea about Anakin, but was more than happy to take advantage once the Jedi found him.

On the other hand, Anakin's discovery really could have been a happy accident, and any plans that either the Jedi or Palpatine had for him came after the fact. If that's the case, then that would have meant we saw a major revision of Palpatine's original strategy in the wake of the events of the Phantom Menace.

As powerful and well-trained as he was, it's unlikely that

19

Darth Maul was ever in Palpatine's long-term plans. Count Dooku also served his purpose as he had the skills to form the Confederacy of Independent Systems and bring it to war against the Jedi and the Republic, but was he always meant to die just as Palpatine's victory was at hand? What course would Palpatine's plan have taken had Anakin not been a part of them?

We may have had a clearer answer to that if we knew exactly when Palpatine decided that Anakin was his go-to guy. Palpatine knew how powerful Anakin would become the moment he met him, but he couldn't know for many years that he would be able to harness it the way Palpatine needed. So while Anakin was on his radar, he may not have been ready to put all his chips in on him just yet.

It's likely that Palpatine saw the possibilities, but didn't decide for sure until the final confrontation between Anakin and Dooku. You need a certain type of ruthlessness to succeed as a Sith Lord, and while Anakin was certainly powerful, Palpatine wouldn't be certain until he saw whether Anakin would dispose of Dooku once he had him at his mercy.

Once he did, Palpatine's decision was made and he revealed himself, tipping off the series of events that led to the destruction of the Jedi and Anakin's transformation into Darth Vader.

Palpatine not only knew about Anakin, but had actually manipulated the Force to create him.

Palpatine revealed a lot more about himself in Revenge of the Sith than we had previously been privy to, and one of those things was the tale he told Anakin of his own master, Darth Plagueis the Wise. Though the focus was obviously on Plagueis' ability to prevent others from dying, Palpatine also mentioned that Plagueis (who had taught his apprentice everything he knew, by the way) was able to manipulate the Force to create life.

This raises the possibility that Palpatine knew all about Anakin because he had created him. While the Jedi were so tied up looking at Anakin's existence as a Force-driven immaculate conception, the reality could be that Palpatine had used Plagueis' ability to create life and was responsible for Anakin even being there in the first place.

If you doubt that, ask yourself how many other Jedi we ever met who were literally conceived by the Force? Anakin is the only one, and the odds of him being the only case of the Force manifesting itself this way seem a little too slim unless there was something (or someone) manipulating the system.

What Happened To Jar Jar Binks After The Fall Of The Jedi?

Before anyone ever set foot in a movie theater to see Phantom Menace for the first time, the one thing we all knew for sure was that we shouldn't get too attached to any new major characters we met during the prequel trilogy. We already knew who was around to play a part in Episode IV, so anyone new we were introduced to would most likely meet their demise by the time the closing credits ran on Episode III.

For the most part, this was true: Qui Gon Jinn, Jango Fett, Count Dooku, General Grievous, Mace Windu, Padme, Shmi Skywalker, and even poor Kit Fisto bit the dust, leaving only the folks we already knew from the original trilogy. Well, there was actually once exception.

Jar Jar Binks survived the violent Clone Wars, the Jedi Purge, and even his own incompetence to become the one and only major prequel trilogy character left standing when all was said and done. There was no ambiguity about his fate: he was clearly seen walking in Padme's funeral procession at the very end of Revenge of the Sith, yet he was nowhere to be found in Episodes IV-VI. How come we never saw hide nor hair of Jar Jar when the story picks back up 20 years later?

The best answer is probably "They had no idea Jar Jar Binks was going to exist when they made the original movies, and they were just as happy to not have to go back and add him in just to keep the continuity." But since that's not a very fun answer, let's look at some of the other possibilities that don't hinge on inconsistent storytelling:

Jar Jar knew who Palpatine really was and why the Jedi were wiped out, but still continued to serve in the Galactic Senate until the time it was dissolved in

Episode IV.

Though Palpatine had reorganized the Republic into the First Galactic Empire in Episode III, the Galactic Senate continued to exist as the Imperial Senate until being dissolved during Episode IV, as Grand Moff Tarkin noted while meeting with other Imperial military leaders on the Death Star. Being the goodhearted, duty-driven creature that he was, Jar Jar may very well have continued serving in the Senate even once everyone else had realized it had become a powerless puppet body controlled by the Emperor.

Unlike the other, more heroic good guys in the saga, Jar Jar could have just decided that enough was enough once that happened. He had lived through some extraordinarily dangerous situations in Episode I, and that may have been enough to convince him that he had done his part and didn't need to risk his neck anymore. He would have simply gone about his business as he previously had until Stormtroopers boarded up the Senate building and left him out of a job.

We're all accustomed to seeing movie heroes like the Jedi who are all in until the end, but remember that Jar Jar was established as a coward right from the moment we met him. He was running for his life when Obi Wan and Qui Gonn first found him on Naboo, and when put in charge of the Gungan army during the Battle of Naboo, he actually surrendered to the droid army before the problem solved itself when Anakin blew up the control ship. Jar Jar did what he had to do to survive, but he was never one to go above and beyond if there wasn't a life or death situation forcing him to.

If Jar Jar just did his duty and stayed out of the way, then we may not have seen him in Episodes IV-VI because there was nothing to see. It may not be the most exciting fate, but it's definitely possible given what we knew about him.

Jar Jar knew full well what was happening when the Empire was formed and decided to do something about it.

On the other hand, Jar Jar had spent enough time around the Jedi that he very well might have known exactly who the Sith were and what was at stake if they were allowed to maintain control of the galaxy. Jar Jar may have even realized how Palpatine had manipulated him into calling for the Senate to grant him the war powers he never set aside. Jar Jar wasn't very bright, but once Palpatine had exposed his true nature, Jar Jar could have connected the dots and realized that he was responsible for the way things had turned out.

Once he came to that realization, Jar Jar may have decided that, since he created the problem, he would have to be the one to solve it. There would be very little he would be able to do openly as a Senator without risking his neck, so Jar Jar could have worked in secret and led an underground resistance that eventually grew into the very same Rebellion that later included Luke, Leia, Han, and the rest.

This is an intriguing possibility since we always knew what the Rebellion was, but never heard anything about its history prior to Episode IV. We knew who was in the group at the time of the original trilogy, but we didn't know who the founding fathers or key members of the past were. There was never any link made between Jar Jar and the Rebellion in the movies, but he would have been one of the few in a position to spearhead such a movement.

An association with the Rebellion could also explain why Jar Jar didn't survive until the original trilogy if his subversive activities got him killed before Episode IV began. The Empire would obviously want to stomp out any anti-Imperial movements before they had a chance to build momentum, and dusting one of their leaders would be an effective way of sending a message to other would-be heroes. If the blind luck that got Jar Jar through Episode I ran out and the Empire got ahold of him, then there might be a Jar Jar-shaped burn outline on an alley wall somewhere on Coruscant.

Jar Jar may have realized how bad things were about to become, and went into hiding while the getting was good.

Though Jar Jar exhibited an extraordinary lack of brains, talent, skill, or any other redeeming qualities, the one thing he did have going for him was a remarkable ability to hide from danger. After hearing that the Jedi had been wiped out, the Republic was being replaced by a dictatorship, and the Senate chamber had been torn to pieces by a fight between two anonymous wizards, Jar Jar may have decided it was time to get out of Dodge.

It would be the smart move, especially since the Emperor was obviously familiar with Jar Jar and his connection to the Jedi. Palpatine had already started taking out anyone else who could implicate him in the Purge once the Jedi were out of the way, having Anakin take out Count Dooku on the Confederate ship and the leaders of the Trade Federation on Mustafar. If the Emperor decided he was next, Jar Jar would want to be as far from Coruscant as he could get.

Don't forget, even Yoda and Obi Wan had gone into hiding rather than face the wrath of Emperor Palpatine, and both stayed off the radar for twenty years until Luke and Leia came of age. If the last two remaining Jedi Masters were averse to showing their faces, nobody could really take issue with Jar Jar doing the same.

Jar Jar had no idea what was going on and continued naively bumbling through life as he always had.

As ridiculous as this may seem given the sweeping changes that took place, Jar Jar may have legitimately had no idea what was going on and never even thought to question why the Chancellor was now a shadowy recluse, why the Republic became an Empire, or why the Jedi all suddenly disappeared. He was never the sharpest knife in the drawer, and he proved how dangerously oblivious he could be when Palpatine manipulated him in Attack of the Clones.

If Jar Jar was still off in his own little world by the time Episode IV rolled around, it's probably better for everyone involved that he stayed out of the way. He had already proven himself to be a major liability by getting caught stealing the raw meat from the street vendor on Tatooine, getting in a fight with Sebulba, and getting his tongue caught in Anakin's pod, and that's just in Episode I. He got all of five minutes of screen time in Episode II, but that was just enough to be responsible for the Republic transforming into a dictatorship.

Bottom line: Jar Jar's involvement never caused anything but headaches for the Jedi. Whatever the reason, his absence was probably a good thing, and that's something you'd probably be hard pressed to find any longtime fans of the original trilogy disagreeing with.

Who Knew Darth Vader's True Identity?

Anakin Skywalker, once a great and powerful Jedi Knight thought to be the Chosen One who would bring balance to the Force, eventually turned to the Dark Side and became the feared, masked Sith Lord known as Darth Vader. Vader once told his son Luke that the name "Anakin Skywalker" no longer had any meaning to him, but it seemed like he wasn't the only one who had left it in the past.

While Obi Wan Kenobi and Yoda were fully aware of Vader's background, it seemed like the general public, including Vader's children Luke and Leia, were in the dark as it related to the mysterious warrior's origins. While that's probably to be expected since most people probably weren't familiar with the Jedi on an individual basis, there was an inner circle who may or may not have known Darth Vader's true identity depending on how well-informed they were.

Uncle Owen & Aunt Beru

Let's start with the most obvious suspects: while Owen and Beru obviously knew that Luke was Anakin's son, did they know who Anakin had become? It's not likely they did, because if they knew that his father was a vengeful Sith Lord, there probably wouldn't have been any way that they would have agreed to take Luke in, family or no.

For one, there was always the possibility, however remote, that Vader would one day come looking for his kid. Owen and Beru weren't heroes, they were poor subsistence farmers squeaking out a living on a crappy planet on the outskirts of the galaxy. Even if Obi Wan had given his personal guarantee that they would be kept safe (which, as we found out in Episode IV, they absolutely weren't), they would have been crazy to agree to take Luke in if they knew what had become of his father.

Also, they would have constantly had the possibility that Luke would turn out like his father hanging over their heads. Owen and Beru may not have known just how far Anakin had fallen, but they did seem to have some idea that Anakin's life had taken him in a bad direction. They weren't very good about concealing their fear that Luke would seek out a similar path, and tried pretty hard to guide Luke away from seeking Obi Wan out after C-3PO and R2-D2 showed up.

While they may not have known everything, Owen and Beru seemed to know enough to be fearful of letting Luke get involved with Obi Wan since he might follow him on one of his damn fool idealistic crusades like his father had.

Senator Bail Organa

Senator Organa definitely knew more about Anakin's fate than most did since he had agreed to take on Anakin's daughter Leia and raise her as his own. But did he know that Anakin had been reborn as Darth Vader following the battle on Mustafar? That's debatable.

While Senator Organa seemed to be a trusted associate, the Jedi weren't a group who were especially prone to letting outsiders into the fold. Much like Owen and Beru, it seems most likely that he knew enough to agree to keep Leia safe from the Empire, but not enough to realize that the baby girl he had agreed to raise belonged to Emperor Palpatine's personal enforcer.

Grand Moff Tarkin

Governor Tarkin and the rest of the senior officials who were present on the Death Star knew that Darth Vader had use of the Force, as we saw when he used it to torture the official who questioned his abilities. However, that's not to say they connected Vader's emergence with the sudden disappearance of Anakin Skywalker after the Jedi were wiped out. From their perspective, they probably assumed that Anakin had been killed during the Jedi Purge and never realized that he and Vader were one and the same.

Jar Jar Binks

Much like Senator Organa, Jar Jar Binks was an associate of the Jedi (albeit for many less good reasons than Organa), and not privy to their internal discussions or information. As we saw in the last chapter, Jar Jar may or may not have even been cognizant of the true nature of the changes the Republic had undergone during its transformation into the Empire. Jar Jar did know Anakin, but he probably wasn't bright enough to connect him with Darth Vader.

Chewbacca

Until we saw Revenge of the Sith, nobody would have suspected that Chewbacca was anything more than a spacefaring smuggler's copilot. However, our perception of Chewie's history was irrevocably altered once we discovered that he was actually the leader of the Wookie army on Kashyyyk during the Clone Wars.

We still have no idea how he wound up with Han Solo, but it was now obvious that he was a lot more deeply involved in the events that led to the rise of the Empire than we had ever suspected. But even still, did he know Anakin before he turned to the Dark Side or realize who he had become once the Sith took over?

It's doubtful that he did, not just because Chewie also fell into the category of "Jedi Associate" like the Lars and Organa families, but also because he would have been cut off from any discussion of Anakin's fate once Yoda left for Coruscant. There's no way we can know for sure since we know so little about the course Chewbacca's life followed between the war on Kashyyyk and his association with Han Solo, but he would most likely have been on the outside looking in without Yoda serving as his information source.

Why Didn't Yoda Take A More Active Role In The Empire Strikes Back?

To the surprise of many who were only familiar with the frail-looking creature we first met when Luke journeyed to Dagobah to complete his training, Yoda took a very active role in the prequel trilogy. He didn't just restrict himself to single combat against fearsome opponents like Count Dooku and Emperor Palpatine, either: he was right in the thick of the battle on Kashyyyk and joined Obi Wan in the liberation of the Jedi Temple.

But that brings us back to the fact that the Yoda we saw in the Empire Strikes Back and Return of the Jedi carefully avoided becoming directly involved in the conflict. He sure as hell didn't offer to come along and help when he warned Luke that only a fully-trained Jedi could hope to defeat Darth Vader. Why would Yoda suddenly be so reluctant to get involved with the effort to destroy his sworn enemies?

It's never easy to tell what on Yoda's mind, but in this case it probably boils down to one (or possibly all) of the following:

Yoda realized he wasn't powerful enough to defeat either the Emperor or Darth Vader.

Let's not mince words: when Yoda fought Palpatine on Coruscant after the Jedi Purge began, he lost. With Mace Windu dead and Anakin Skywalker turned to the Dark Side, Yoda was the only Jedi left who was powerful enough to have a shot at taking Palpatine out. Yoda knew it had to be him: no other Jedi could hope to destroy the Sith Lord, and he told Obi Wan as much before sending him after Anakin.

But with the fate of both the Republic and the Jedi Order riding on the outcome of that battle, Yoda couldn't get the job done. Palpatine was too strong, overpowering him with Sith lightning and using the Force to throw pieces of the Senate chamber at his adversary. Yoda knew he couldn't win, and headed for the hills to avoid the same fate that Mace Windu had met.

As we know, Yoda went into hiding and, by the time the events of the original trilogy rolled around, was old and feeble. Sure, he may still have had enough command of the Force to do tricks like pulling Luke's ship out of the swamp, but as we saw when Obi Wan fought Vader on the Death Star, you don't get stronger as you hit your twilight years.

Yoda may have let the Fall of the Jedi creep up on him, but by the time Luke sought him out, he knew that he no longer had command of the kind of power it would take to defeat the Emperor or Darth Vader.

An opening to get close enough to the Emperor and Vader to try and destroy them never presented itself.

That then raises the question of why Yoda didn't take another shot at killing Palpatine while he was still young enough to try. He wouldn't have had to worry about Anakin's kids, Obi Wan and Senator Organa had them covered, so it should have been a priority for Yoda to go back after the Emperor before things got too out of hand, right?

Well, it turns out that things might have actually gotten too far out of hand long before the Fall of the Jedi. Getting another chance to fight the Emperor was more than a matter of just walking back into his office and waving his guards off the way he had the first time. Palpatine had let his guard down because he thought all the Jedi were exterminated after issuing Order 66, and that wasn't a mistake he was about to make a second time.

Remember, Palpatine had been granted emergency wartime powers and had ruled the Republic as a virtual dictator for over a decade by the time the Jedi fell. That's a long time to build up a power base, and by the time the Jedi were wiped out, Palpatine's reach extended across virtually the entire galaxy. He had eyes and ears (and boots) everywhere, and those are odds that even Yoda would have had a hard time overcoming.

Yoda would have never gotten close to the Emperor, and would have been lucky to even get very far from Dagobah before he was spotted. There's no way he would have been able to singlehandedly fight his way back into the Imperial capital AND defeat the Emperor with every stormtrooper in the galaxy out to get him.

He planned all along to rely on the Skywalker twins to not only destroy the Empire, but rebuild the Jedi Order.

Then there was the matter of restoring the Jedi Order that Yoda had dedicated his life to. The Jedi had been nearly wiped out by the Sith, the Jedi Temple and all the treasures it contained left in ruins, and Imperial forces ordered to kill any remaining Jedi on sight, but Yoda still held out hope that the Jedi Order would one day be restored to its former glory.

But even if the Sith were somehow defeated, Yoda knew he wouldn't live long enough to take a personal hand in rebuilding the Jedi Order. In fact, he didn't even live long enough to see the Emperor destroyed and Anakin redeemed, dying of natural causes just before the final series of battles ensued. Yoda probably realized that the time left to him would be better spent ensuring the survival of the Jedi, hence his interest in protecting Luke and Leia.

Even if Yoda had left Dagobah and managed to kill Vader and the Emperor, the unique set of circumstances that led the

Skywalker twins to becoming leaders and heroes in their own right never would have happened. Luke and Leia both would have lived and died without ever learning their true heritage or having a chance to explore the potential they realized during the Rebellion.

All parents struggle with letting their kids learn to handle themselves and learn from their own mistakes, rather than swooping in and solving all their problems for them. Given that their mother was dead and their father had become a tyrannical Dark Lord of the Sith, the Jedi became the closest thing Luke and Leia had to family, and it fell to Yoda to make those choices.

The difference here, however, is that the outcome of his choices weren't a matter of whether Luke and Leia would wind up on a psychiatrist's couch someday, though they probably did anyway given everything they lived through. No, the survival of the Jedi was as stake, and as difficult as it may have been for Yoda to stay out of the way and let the chips fall where they may, he knew it was the best thing to do if he didn't want the Jedi Order to die with him.

Why Weren't Yoda And Obi-Wan Honest With Luke About His Family History?

One of the most famously shocking moments in not just the Star Wars saga, but in all of movie history, was when Luke Skywalker discovered that Darth Vader was his father at the end of Empire Strikes Back. We weren't the only ones caught off guard by that, as Obi Wan Kenobi had told Luke that Vader had betrayed and murdered Anakin Skywalker even though the truth was that he had actually BECOME him.

Luke was understandably upset when he found out that he had been lied to, and wasn't buying Obi Wan's "certain point of view" logic. You couldn't really blame Luke for being mad, and we had to wonder why Obi Wan and Yoda didn't tell Luke the truth before Vader did. They had to know that Vader would spill the beans when they came face to face, right? Wouldn't it have made sense to come clean before Vader made them look like a couple of liars?

That would seem like a logical question to ask, but Yoda was always thinking a few moves ahead and may have had some legitimate reasons not to reveal Luke's heritage up front...

They weren't expecting him to confront Vader so soon.

It may be that Yoda and Obi Wan fully intended to reveal everything to Luke when they decided he was ready to know the truth, but then the events on Bespin disrupted that plan. I think this is what most people probably assumed, and the nature of the conversation when Luke decided to drop everything and go rescue his friends seems to confirm that.

Luke made his desire to train in the ways of the Force clear when he first approached Yoda, so it must have been a pretty big shock to both of the elder Jedi when Luke just picked up and left the way he did. They may not have expected him to develop his Jedi senses well enough to detect the danger his friends were in so quickly, but it seemed apparent that they expected to have more time to train him before he went running off to face Vader.

In retrospect, that may have been a good time to change their plans and tell Luke the truth even if they weren't sure he was ready. They both knew full well how Anakin's impulsiveness had led him astray, and that same impulsiveness could have gotten Luke killed or worse if he didn't know what he was walking into. But then again, Yoda and Obi Wan may still have been unwilling to tell Luke the truth because...

They were hoping he would destroy Vader before he found out who he was.

Obi Wan and Yoda knew who Luke was, they knew who Vader really was, and they knew that Luke didn't know who Vader really was. Unfortunately for them, they may not have been aware that Vader had figured out who Luke was and had become obsessed with trying to find and reconnect with his estranged son.

If they didn't realize that Vader knew his son was alive, then they may have kept their mouths shut because they were hoping that Luke would destroy Vader before he found out the truth. Yoda and Obi Wan would have known it was a longshot since Luke was still a novice in the ways of the Jedi, but due to Luke's strong natural affinity with the Force, they may have hoped he would defy the odds and defeat Vader before the truth came out.

On the other hand, if things went south and Luke was either turned to the Dark Side or killed, Yoda and Obi Wan did still have a backup plan...

They knew they had Leia to fall back on if Luke turned or was killed.

Most people probably wouldn't consider this characteristic of the way Yoda or Obi Wan would operate, but they might have assumed that Luke would get himself killed if he went after Vader, and wrote him off as a lost cause the instant he decided to leave. They may have even considered Luke expendable since they still had a chance to use Leia to destroy the Sith if her brother couldn't swing it, and Yoda's "No, there is another" comment seems to suggest that this was their mentality as they watched Luke blast off from Dagobah.

This may not be the most charitable way to think of Yoda or Obi Wan, but it was clear that the Jedi considered the safety of Anakin's children to be of paramount importance from the moment they were born. Don't kid yourself by thinking that this was out of the goodness of their hearts: they hoped that one day, Anakin's offspring would be powerful enough to challenge their father and bring down the Empire that they had themselves failed to destroy.

Bottom line: Luke and Leia were protected for one reason only, and that's to be used as surrogates for the Jedi once they were old enough to bring their power to bear against the Sith. It was a stroke of luck that Padme happened to be carrying twins, because this meant that they had a second chance if one of them failed.

Here's an even more shocking possibility: what if Yoda and Obi Wan knew from the beginning that Luke would fail when he faced Vader on Bespin, and were planning for Leia to be the one to destroy Vader all along? Is it possible that they had used Luke as a dry run so they could work out the kinks in the plan before sending Leia into the fray? Or maybe they intentionally sent Luke to his death so that Vader would be caught off guard by

Leia after he assumed he no longer had any living children?

Yoda and Obi Wan's ultimate goal was to destroy the Sith and restore the Jedi Order, so however they saw Luke and Leia fitting into that plan, there's a good chance they would have gone forward without hesitation or concern for them as individuals. Remember, Yoda actually told Luke to stay on Dagobah and let his friends suffer for the greater good, so I don't think it's a stretch to believe that he would have sacrificed the Skywalkers if he had to. In that regard, does that willingness to use even the closest of associates as pawns make Yoda any different from Emperor Palpatine?

Why Didn't Vader Realize Leia Was His Daughter?

Much of the original trilogy focused on Darth Vader's obsession with finding and subverting Luke Skywalker, the son he thought had died with Padme all those years ago. Vader figured out who Luke was after he sensed his connection with the Force during the Battle of Yavin at the end of Episode IV, and was able to divine not only his thoughts, but even his mere presence when the rebels tried sneaking onto the forest moon of Endor in Return of the Jedi.

Strangely, Vader never had any clue that Leia was also his child until Luke's thoughts betrayed him during their final battle on the Second Death Star. The whole subject of Vader and Leia's relationship really seemed to get glossed over, with Leia barely batting an eye when Luke spilled the family history to her in the Ewok Village. But that aside, Vader and Leia's conversation at the beginning of Episode IV suggested that they were very familiar with one another, so it's fair to ask how Vader never figured out her true identity on his own.

How could Leia have avoided detection while right under Vader's nose for all those years? Well...

Leia wasn't as strong with the Force as Luke thought she was.

This seems a likely possibility since Luke's strength with the Force was what tipped Vader off to his identity to begin with. He couldn't have known who he was just because he used the Force, he could have just been any other Force-wielding kid Obi Wan had trained. Vader knew exactly who Luke was, and the Force was how he fingerprinted him.

It then follows that if Leia had any use of the Force, or at least a strong enough affinity to make her a viable alternative if Luke failed (as Yoda seemed to believe), how could Vader have missed that? He was as Force-sensitive as anyone, yet he had no clue that the girl he was interrogating with evil needle droids was his daughter.

If Leia the same kind of power as her brother, Vader would have sensed it immediately and realized her true identity years before Episode IV began. An entire chapter in this book covers reasons why Leia probably didn't have any use of the Force, and that would explain Vader's inability to sense her true identity.

Yoda used the Force to hide Luke and Leia from Vader.

This may be a longshot, but if anyone could pull it off, it'd be Yoda. After all, he was able to hide his own massive Force presence and avoid discovery for years after the Jedi Purge. In fact, he lived out the rest of his life without ever being found by Vader and Palpatine, so if he was able to stay off the radar for all that time, it would stand to reason that he might be able to do the same for Luke and Leia.

Remember, separating the twins and hiding them from Vader was his idea to begin with. He knew he couldn't let them be discovered before they were old enough to survive on their own, otherwise they'd either be killed to prevent them from becoming a problem later on, or more likely, subverted to the Dark Side as their father had been.

But merely separating and hiding them wouldn't be enough, because if Vader were to somehow discover them before the time was right, there would be no way Owen and Beru, Senator Organa, or Obi Wan would be able to protect them from the might of the Imperial Army, much less Darth Vader himself. Yoda would have known he couldn't leave that to chance, and since we had seen him do some pretty wild things with the Force, he may have had a way to cast some protective shroud over them to obscure their presence while they grew up.

Palpatine used the Force to hide Luke and Leia from Vader.

In the earlier chapter about whether Vader realized Palpatine lied about Padme's fate, we looked at the possibility that Palpatine knew Anakin's children had survived and intentionally withheld that knowledge from Vader. If that were the case, perhaps Palpatine had as big a hand in protecting them from being discovered by their father as Yoda, albeit for completely different, much less altruistic reasons.

Unlike Yoda, who would have used the Force from a distance to veil the twins from Vader, Palpatine was a constant presence in Vader's life. Rather than use the Force to hide Luke and Leia across the vast reaches of space, he could instead cloud Vader's mind from close proximity, and "muffle" his ability to use the Force to sense his children. His ability to manipulate Vader was well documented, so this would have been par for the course.

If this was Palpatine's doing, then it's absolutely feasible that Vader could stand face-to-face with his own daughter and never be the wiser. Luke's outburst of Force usage during the Battle of Yavin would have been powerful enough to shine through Palpatine's veil, but since Leia never had occasion to use her own Force powers (assuming they existed at all), nothing about her would have ever stood out to Vader the way Luke did.

Were Vader and Obi Wan Aware Of Each Other's Survival Before Their Meeting On The Death Star?

After spending most of their lives fighting the forces of evil together, Anakin Skywalker and Obi Wan Kenobi had a falling out and fought one another in an epic battle on the volcanic planet of Mustafar. That battle resulted in Anakin's mutilation and rebirth as the masked Darth Vader, while Obi Wan went into hiding and spent years avoiding discovery by the Empire.

Anakin and Obi Wan didn't cross paths again for many years, but finally met one last time on the Death Star when Obi Wan led the mission to rescue Princess Leia from the Empire. They engaged in their final battle, and Obi Wan sacrificed himself to give Luke and Leia a chance to escape Vader's clutches.

Vader had finally destroyed his old master, but facing him at all was clearly not something the ex-Jedi had expected when he got up that morning. In fact, Grand Moff Tarkin seemed surprised at the suggestion that Obi Wan was even still alive, suggesting that Obi Wan was generally thought to have been long dead by the time he finally reappeared.

By that same token, Anakin was short two arms and two legs the last time Obi Wan had seen him, and had burst into flames as what was left of his body slid toward the hot lava bubbling below. It seemed inconceivable that anyone could have survived that, even Anakin, and indeed Obi Wan looked quite surprised when he finally came face-to-face with his former apprentice on the Death Star.

Both men had good reason to assume the other was dead, but there were also plenty of reasons for each to believe the other had survived. They had fought side-by-side for years, and each knew how tough the other was. In spite of the reasons to believe otherwise, would either man really be all that surprised to discover the other was still alive?

Let's try and answer that by considering the likelihood of the following possible scenarios:

Obi Wan had no idea Anakin had survived Mustafar.

This seems like a reasonable conclusion to come to given the condition Anakin was in when Obi Wan left him on Mustafar. Obi Wan may have assumed Anakin was done for, and probably would have finished him right then and there had he known Anakin would survive. With his focus on watching over Luke at the time, Obi Wan may not have even been thinking about what the Sith were doing, at least not yet.

Remember, the whole idea behind bringing Luke to Tatooine in the first place was that it was a remote location outside the Empire's sphere of influence. That also placed Tatooine outside the typical reach of news about current events, so it's possible that Obi Wan was so cut off enough from society during his exile on Tatooine that he never found out Anakin survived, or at least didn't for a really long time.

Obi Wan knew Anakin was alive and had become Darth Vader.

All that being said, it's probably unlikely that Obi Wan was caught completely unawares when he ran into Vader on the Death Star. We don't know that Obi Wan never left Tatooine after the fall of the Jedi, and if he had dared to venture into Imperial territory, it's a good bet that he would have spent some time catching up on current affairs.

Once he did, he would have discovered that Emperor Palpatine suddenly had a masked enforcer, who happened to have an extremely strong command of the Force, working for him. At that point, it wouldn't have been much of a stretch for Obi Wan to do the math and figure out this mysterious warrior's true identity.

Vader assumed Obi Wan was dead.

The only reasonable explanation for why anyone might have thought Obi Wan was dead by the time Episode IV happened is that he would have been old enough to die by natural causes. While that may seem reasonable to anyone without knowledge of the Force, it's hard to believe that Vader would have been satisfied and left it at that.

Vader knew Obi Wan was alive and still out there somewhere.

Unlike his former apprentice, Obi Wan walked away from the battle on Mustafar in one piece. He was nowhere to be found after that confrontation, but even with the certainty that Vader would have torn the galaxy apart looking for his former master, he would have never found anything to indicate that Obi Wan was dead.

Obviously, this was because Obi Wan was still very much alive and hiding out on Vader's former home planet of Tatooine. Though his inability to find Obi Wan may have caused him to scale back his search and focus on other priorities, Vader would have never been convinced that the matter was settled until he saw conclusive evidence of Obi Wan's death.

Until then, he would have lived with a certainty that Obi Wan was alive and that he would have to face him again before all was said and done. While Vader couldn't be a hundred percent certain that Obi Wan was alive, he probably had a pretty good idea that he was.

How Did Luke's Lightsaber Get From Bespin To Maz Kanata's Basement?

When Darth Vader cut off Luke Skywalker's lightsaber hand to end their duel on Cloud City, the lightsaber fell into the great chasm below and appeared to be lost forever. Luke threw himself into the chasm as well to escape Vader, but when he landed at the bottom of the shaft, the lightsaber was nowhere to be found.

Luke was unceremoniously dumped out the bottom of the shaft and eventually rescued by the crew of the Millennium Falcon. After being fitted with an artificial right hand, Luke set about constructing a new lightsaber, which he wielded in his next duel with Vader on the Second Death Star.

Luke 's original lightsaber, which had been Anakin's before him, was apparently lost after the escape from Bespin. We had no idea where it could have ended up: did it get dumped out the same shaft Luke did, tumbling into the gaseous planet below? Did it go down a different shaft and land where someone might find it? Could it have taken another path we wouldn't even think to explore?

Against all odds, the long lost Skywalker lightsaber finally reappeared in Maz Kanata's basement on Takodana. Maz Kanata told Han Solo that the story of how she came into possession of such an artifact would have to wait for another time, but for right now, let's consider the possibility that...

Luke himself went back for it and then entrusted it to Maz Kanata.

While Luke constructed his own lightsaber to replace the one he had lost on Bespin, that could just have been because he needed one in a hurry for his next confrontation with Darth

Vader. Luke would have had a lot more time on his hands once the battle with the Empire was no longer consuming all of his attention, and may have gone back to Bespin to search for his lost family heirloom in the years that followed.

Why would Luke have done this? Possibly because of sentimental value, since it had belonged to his father before him. Since Vader was dead and any possessions he may have had probably went up with the Second Death Star, Luke may have wanted to retrieve it for himself or, if he ever had any, his own children.

Luke may also have wanted to make sure it didn't fall into the wrong hands since lightsabers are dangerous, and distinctive, weapons. As the Grand Master of the New Jedi Order, the last thing he would have needed would be the blame for some criminal getting ahold of his lightsaber and using it for nefarious purposes.

The problem with this theory is why Luke would have put the time and effort into finding the lightsaber only to turn it over to Maz Kanata. We could have a better idea once we learn a little more about her own background, but given that her basement would be about the last place anyone would think to look for it, that might make it the perfect place for Luke to ensure it stayed hidden until its next bearer was ready to take it up.

Someone else who knew where it had been lost went to Bespin and recovered it.

This would, of course, be dependent on someone even knowing that Luke had lost it in the first place and where, and very few people did. The only people who might have known would have been Luke, Leia, Han, Lando, Chewbacca, C-3PO, R2-D2, and Darth Vader, and if any of Luke's friends had recovered it, they would have almost certainly returned it to him.

That leaves the intriguing possibility that Darth Vader himself actually returned to Cloud City after it had been evacuated, and recovered his own lightsaber that had been lost to him since his battle with Obi-Wan on Mustafar. He certainly would have recognized it the moment Luke brought it to bear in their first battle, and could have made a point of recovering his lost property afterward.

If Vader had reclaimed his old lightsaber, then it would have almost certainly been kept in the Imperial capital on Coruscant, his personal Star Destroyer, or some other Imperial facility until the end of the war. As with most wars, those facilities were likely looted to the bone as soon as the Empire raised the white flag.

If that happened, then some scavenger probably made off with the lightsaber without even realizing what they had in their possession. Maz Kanata, being the connoisseur of unusual artifacts such as she was, would have been far better equipped to recognize its significance, and would have happily taken it off the scavenger's hands, likely for far less than its actual value.

It turned up as a matter of blind luck.

As unlikely as it seems, the lightsaber could have just found its way to Maz Kanata's by pure coincidence. Even if Luke and Vader never tried to find it (or had, but were unsuccessful), the winds of fate may have still somehow conveyed the lightsaber back into the middle of the action just as everything started breaking down again.

So how might the lightsaber have gotten to Takodana in this case? Who knows? Cloud City was a mining colony, so it could have wound up on some scrap heap that was eventually claimed by someone who brought it through Maz Kanata's neck of the woods.

If it fell out the same shaft Luke did and tumbled downward into Bespin's atmosphere, it could at some point have launched out of its orbit and been picked up by someone who, once again, ended up on Takodana.

Whatever actually happened, the "pure luck" theory pretty much relies on the likelihood that whoever wound up in possession of the lightsaber eventually brought it to Takodana. That doesn't seem like such a longshot since the place seemed like a pretty popular destination for transients of all kinds, so however unlikely a coincidence like this seems, it is at least plausible.

The lightsaber itself had enough of a Force imprint that it was able to find its way somewhere it would be found.

In the Lord of the Rings, Sauron's One Ring was not merely a powerful weapon to be wielded by others. It was practically a living being in its own right, with a will of its own and the intelligence to pass itself from one holder to the next as it slowly made its way back to its rightful owner, Sauron.

Though we had never previously seen a lightsaber exhibit any such ability, the fact that Luke's actually called out to Rey and showed her the visions suggests that there might be more to them than meets the eye. Could lightsabers be imbued with some kind of sentience by their creators in the same way the One Ring was?

It's definitely possible, since the ability to construct a lightsaber seems to be regarded as the certifying mark of someone who has mastered use of the Force. Why would assembling what appears to be just a piece of technology, albeit a powerful one, seem so impressive to people who could lift a train with the power of their minds, unless there was an element to the process that only a master of the Force could provide?

If part of the process of crafting a lightsaber involves channeling your Force energy into the new weapon, then it may very well receive some spiritual imprint that not only "awakens" it, but also uniquely binds it to its owner. If that's the case, then a lightsaber may very well have the same ability to find its way home that the One Ring does.

So if that's the case, then why wouldn't it have tried to find its way back to Darth Vader during the years it was in Obi-Wan's possession? Perhaps Luke carried enough of Anakin Skywalker's Force imprint that it tricked the lightsaber into thinking its owner was nearby all along when, in reality, he was very, very far away.

Why that lightsaber would then react to Rey also figures into our next unsolved mystery...

Who is Rey, And What Happened To Her Family?

One of the biggest mysteries coming out of Episode VII is who exactly Rey is, who her family was, and what happened to them after leaving her on Jakku. The vision sequence after she picked up Luke's lightsaber showed us that she was brought to Jakku when she was a young child, and despite their promise to return for her, Rey never saw her family again.

Whoever Rey's family is, it's likely they'll turn out to be important since the vision suggests that she was left on Jakku for her own protection. It wouldn't be the first time that had happened in a Star Wars movie, since Luke and Leia were hidden from Darth Vader as infants.

It would also seem likely that Rey's family had some affinity with the Force that was then passed down to Rey. Could they have hidden Rey because their strength with the Force made them (and Rey by proxy) targets, and they didn't want her to wind up in harm's way until she had mastered her powers?

The fact that Rey's family never returned for her would indicate that whatever they were running from finally caught up with them. Since they weren't around to give us the answers themselves, let's run through the different possibilities...

Rey is Luke Skywalker's daughter.

This seems to be the fan favorite theory, and it makes sense given some of the clues we got during Episode VII. Specifically, the most popular theory is that she is Luke Skywalker's long lost daughter who has now come of age and begun to discover her power.

The big neon sign pointing us in this direction is

obviously the fact that the lightsaber that once belonged to Anakin and then Luke Skywalker began calling out to her. Merely touching it caused Rey to see visions of the past that she had an unusually traumatic emotional response to.

Also, it seems like a pretty big coincidence that Maz just happened to wander down there and begin pushing Rey to take the lightsaber after the visions ceased. Remember, Maz had asked Han who she was, but the scene cut elsewhere before we heard Han's answer.

This exchange also suggests that Han knew more than he was letting on, and if he knew Luke had a daughter, it's possible that he began to put the pieces together pretty early on. Whatever he told Maz, it caused her to follow Rey downstairs and offer her Luke's lightsaber after holding onto it in secret for many years.

Also pointing us to this conclusion is the fact that, while reading her mind, Kylo Ren discovered a mental image of a solitary island in the middle of an ocean. Where does Rey find Luke at the end of the movie? That's right, on a solitary island in the middle of an ocean.

Could this place Luke's been hiding out be Rey's original home? Why else would a girl who spent most of her life on a desert planet, then landed on Takodana and said she never knew there was that much green in the galaxy, have a vision of an island in an ocean if it were a landscape she had never seen before?

Rey is Han and Leia's daughter.

What if Rey is a Skywalker, but is actually Han and Leia's child instead of Luke's? She would certainly resemble both her mother and grandmother in their youths if that were true, so could she have gotten her Force powers through Leia's side of the family?

Though Leia apparently never explored her own Force powers (which we'll cover in more depth later on), it was pretty well established that Luke, Obi Wan, and Yoda all believed she carried the same power Luke did. Ben, as Kylo Ren, obviously exhibited great strength with the Force, so it's likely that Rey would have the potential for the same kind of power if she were his sister.

If that's the case, then it would explain why Han, who had become an extremely grumpy old man in the thirty years since the Empire fell, softened up to her so quickly. It could also be why he was so quick to offer her a job on the Millennium Falcon and teach her how to use a blaster.

The loss of their son Ben to the Dark Side obviously drove enough of a wedge between Han and Leia that Han left Leia and never returned. Is it possible that, fearing she could go down the same path as her brother, Han dropped his daughter on Jakku on his way out of town?

This theory would explain a lot, but there are a few inconsistencies that would seem to contradict this theory. For one, neither Han nor Leia came right out and told Rey they were her parents. It's possible they would have resisted doing so for fear of Kylo Ren and Snoke discovering her, but that would have been a moot point by then for a couple of reasons.

For one, Kylo Ren would know he had a little sister who mysteriously vanished one day. He seems like a smart enough guy that, if he one day ran into a Force-wielding girl around the age his sister would be, who was hanging out with his father no less, he'd probably put the pieces together pretty quickly. That's also assuming he wouldn't have learned her true identity while reading her mind.

Also, any need to protect Rey by hiding her from Snoke and Kylo Ren would have gone out the window once she started flying the Millennium Falcon around to carry a droid back to

Resistance HQ, and certainly by the time she DEFEATED Kylo Ren in a lightsaber battle. If they were ever going to reveal a family relation, Leia would certainly have done it after Rey returned from Starkiller Base, and before she went off looking for Luke.

Then again, Han may not have said anything because she wasn't his daughter after all, like if...

Rey is Leia's daughter, but not Han's.

Han and Leia's reunion made it seem like they had not seen each other in a long, long time. Depending on how long it had been since Han left, is it possible that Leia had Rey with a different father after losing Han and Ben?

If that's the case, then we might not even necessarily need to explore the background of Rey's father to any great degree. He could have been someone in the Resistance or Leia's mailman for all the difference it made, because Rey's important heritage would have come from Leia's side of the family.

But again, we run into the question of why Leia wouldn't have said anything to her. They didn't actually come face-to-face until Rey got back to the Resistance base at the end of the movie, and if Leia really was her mother, it's hard to understand why she wouldn't have said something at that time.

Rey is a Kenobi.

This one would be a bit of a longshot, but this would make her as good as family even if she didn't turn out to be a Skywalker herself. Could Rey have use of the Force because she's descended from Obi-Wan Kenobi?

You would think we would have some knowledge of Obi-Wan having a child (or grandchild, since Obi-Wan himself would have been long dead by the time Rey would have been conceived), but it is possible there are things from his past that we haven't been privy to?

Don't forget, the prequel trilogy spanned about twenty years during which Obi-Wan would have been in his child-causing prime. Could some of his travels between prequel movies, or even prior to the events of Episode I, have led to the unexpected conception of a child we never met?

The rules of the Jedi Order would have prohibited any kind of romantic involvement for members of their order. That's why Anakin and Padme kept their marriage secret for so long, almost up until the moment Padme died.

If Obi-Wan did get romantic with someone in a moment of weakness, he very well could have kept the situation quiet for fear of getting kicked out of the Jedi Order himself. If that's the case, it's possible that his child had no idea who their father was, and therefore, neither did Rey. Depending on how things went down, it's possible even the mother of Obi-Wan's child had no idea who he really was.

It's also likely that Obi-Wan would have avoided revealing the existence of a child because he thought they would be in danger if his enemies found out about them. If Rey's parents suddenly found out they were of the Kenobi line because Snoke or Kylo Ren showed up to try and kill them, that would explain why they left her on Jakku and disappeared in such a hurry.

It would also provide a solid alternate explanation as to why she reacted the way she did after touching the lightsaber in Maz Kanata's basement. If you really think about it, she might have actually been far more likely to react to the lightsaber if she were a Kenobi than if she were a Skywalker.

Anakin used that lightsaber for a few years between Episode II and III, then Luke had it for a few between the original movie and Empire Strikes Back. Obi-Wan had it in his possession for over twenty years, far longer than either of its "legitimate" owners, and may have left a trace of his own on it.

Could Episode VIII start with Luke telling Rey that she's the second Kenobi to give him that lightsaber? Will Luke then train Rey in the ways of the Force as her grandfather had done for him all those years ago?

Rey is a descendant of a Sith.

Though the Jedi led (mostly) chaste existences, the Sith were wildly self-indulgent, and held themselves to no such standards. Is it possible that a Sith like Count Dooku or Palpatine fathered a child at some point, and that child in turn produced Rey?

If so, their descendants would carry immense Force power. As I explored in **The Star Wars Book Of Lists**, Dooku and Palpatine were two of the most powerful Force users who ever lived, and any children or grandchildren of theirs would practically be walking barrels of Force TNT.

It also raises another interesting possibility: what if, instead of being hidden for her protection by benevolent parents, she was descended from a grandfather who refused to even acknowledge he fathered a child?

Let's take that line of thought a bit further and throw this one at the wall: what if Rey's parents didn't know who their father was, but Luke Skywalker found out and came after them? It's possible that her parents did try to hide her on Jakku, but to protect her from the Jedi and not the Dark Side as we might be led to believe.

Alternately, what if Luke would have killed her parents, but left her on Jakku himself rather than kill her as well? Luke was a bit gentler than Anakin and far less likely to massacre children, so maybe the idea was to leave her in an isolated environment and see how she turned out?

This would explain why Rey was marooned in such an unforgiving environment. Luke and Leia were hidden with people who would care for them, but Rey was literally left to fend for herself amongst a parade of lowlifes on a desert planet. Seems like a weird place to leave your kid, unless it was Luke who consciously let her where he figured she would be out of the way and unable to become the kind of threat her ancestor had been.

Rey is descended from someone we haven't met.

This is possible, but seems like it would be the least likely to be true. Rey's heritage is such a major mystery that it would be a pretty big letdown if Rey's parents weren't known to us, but we should consider the possibility.

One explanation that could support this idea is that Rey did seem to become very proficient with the Force and lightsaber combat very quickly. Her parents might not be important in and of themselves, but they may have sent her to train with Luke as a small child after discovering she could use the Force, and then after leaving him, the skill remained dormant until the events of Episode VII.

If that's the case, then it could be that her parents found out what happened when Kylo Ren turned on the new Jedi, rescued her somehow, and ran. They obviously would have done whatever they could to save their daughter from whatever fate Kylo Ren had planned for her, so that could lead us to the revelation that Luke knows who she is, even if she doesn't turn out to be his daughter after all.

How Did The Millennium Falcon Wind Up On Jakku?

Aside from being one of the most iconic and recognizable pieces of the Star Wars mythos, the Millennium Falcon was Han Solo's most prized possession. He loved it so much that he could barely stand the idea of leaving it in Lando's hands for the assault on the Second Death Star.

This begs the question: how could the Millennium Falcon have found its way out of the hands of an owner who treasured it as much as Han did? Did it happen through some unforeseeable set of circumstances, or could a good enough reason for Han to part with it willingly have presented itself?

Han is now too dead to tell us himself, so let's see if we can reconstruct the Millennium Falcon's journey to Jakku on our own...

It really had been stolen from Han.

Han seemed pretty adamant, and indignant, about the fact that his legendary ship had been stolen from him. He didn't care who else's hands it had passed through or why Rey and Finn were flying around on it, he still considered it "home."

But given how much the Millennium Falcon meant to him, how could anyone have stolen it in the first place? Wouldn't someone as street smart as Han keep it firmly under lock and key? The Rebellion would have never had a chance without it, so wouldn't the New Republic also want to see to it that the Falcon was taken care of?

Answering that might be easier if we knew what Han did with the ship after the fall of the Empire. It sounded like he settled down with Leia for many years after Endor, so he may not have needed to keep a ship uniquely designed for space battles and smuggling in active service at that time.

If they were living the galactic equivalent of life in suburbia, he may have put it in storage and left it there for who knows how long. It could have been stolen from there at any time, and Han would have had no idea it was gone until he went looking for it on his way out of town.

On the other hand, it seems more likely that it was stolen at some point after he left, especially given some of the people Han was known to deal with. Perhaps he spent a little too long at a place like the Mos Eisley Cantina one night, and gave some space carjacker just enough time to fire the Falcon up and disappear with it.

Han lost it in a game of chance.

Though we never heard the specifics, we do know that Han Solo originally acquired the Millennium Falcon from its prior owner, Lando Calrissian, in some kind of game of chance. Is it possible that he lost it in the same way?

When Han and Chewbacca first crossed paths with Rey and Finn on the Falcon, Han insisted that the ship had been stolen from him. What if it wasn't stolen in the "breaking a window and hotwiring it" sense, but rather that Han had lost it in another game of chance that he believed to have been rigged?

It would seem to fit with what we know about Han's life after leaving Leia and the Resistance. He said he had gone back to the only other life he was ever good at, and while that obviously included smuggling, it could have also included gambling with the dredges of society...dredges who might not be averse to dealing from the bottom of the deck.

It was given to Unkar Plutt as payment for watching

over Rey.

During Rey's vision sequence when we see her being left on Jakku as a child, the hand holding onto her as she cried for her family to come back appeared to match that of Unkar Plutt, the junk buyer and apparent focal point of the economy, such as it was, at Niima Outpost.

To say that Unkar Plutt and Rey didn't exactly have the coziest relationship would be an understatement. Rey doesn't ever appear overly enthusiastic to do business with him, and Plutt doesn't seem especially interested in her welfare either, as long as she keeps bringing him useful scrap found in the skeletons of destroyed Imperial ships.

Why would anyone decide Jakku would be a good place to leave Rey, at the time still a child? More to the point, what would ever move Rey's parents to leave her with someone like Unkar Plutt?

We don't know for sure that it was definitely his arm we saw in the vision, but since nobody else on Jakku seems to match it, we'll assume that it was indeed Unkar Plutt. The guy doesn't seem to be interested in anything other than scrap metal, so why would he even entertain the thought of watching over Rey, even as little as he appeared to be doing so?

Well, the business part might be the key, because if he had been offered the Millennium Falcon, the legendary ship that had famously fought in the Rebellion and helped destroy both Death Stars, what self-respecting junk dealer would say no?

In fact, Unkar Plutt seemed pretty upset when Rey and Finn blasted off in "his" ship as they escaped the First Order's troops. If the ship was the only reason he accepted Rey in the first place, that would explain why.

Lor San Tekka kept it there in the event he and Rey

needed to escape in a hurry.

Staying on the "Millennium Falcon was left on Jakku on purpose" train for another moment, does anyone else think it seemed like a pretty big coincidence that Rey, the Millennium Falcon, and Lor San Tekka (the guy with the map to Luke Skywalker's secret hideout) were all within a day's walk on the same planet?

Princess Leia, Poe Dameron, and Kylo Ren obviously all knew Lor San Tekka very well, but nobody bothered to explain his background to us. Was he a member of the Rebellion? A repentant Imperial official? Someone who had served Leia's family way back on Alderaan?

We don't know, and while we may find out more in the upcoming Anthology movies, there's so little information about the guy that I decided to scrap the chapter I was originally going to dedicate to him in this book.

That said, he's obviously someone important enough to be trusted with Luke Skywalker's most guarded secret. Given that, as well as the fact that he seemed to be a very high-level confidant to Princess Leia, is it possible that Luke's location wasn't the only thing he was entrusted with?

We earlier speculated as to why Rey would be left in the middle of a desert wasteland with a creep like Unkar Plutt as her babysitter. What if Plutt wasn't the one tasked with assuring Rey's well-being, but Lor San Tekka?

In much the same way Obi-Wan Kenobi volunteered to set up shop on Tatooine to watch over Luke, Lor San Tekka may have had the same job with Rey. But while Obi-Wan kept his vigil from a distance, could Lor San Tekka have been a more frequent presence in Rey's life?

It's possible that he and Rey may have actually known

each other very well, and we didn't find out since we never saw them interact during the movie. If so, then Rey might have blasted off of Jakku with no idea that her friend had been cut down by Kylo Ren only a day earlier.

If Lor San Tekka was designated to be Rey's guardian, and the time ever came when he had to get her out of Dodge in a hurry, the Millennium Falcon would have been the perfect ship to escape in. It could easily outrun any ship in the First Order's fleet, and did so when Rey, Finn, and BB-8 made their escape.

Why Did Kylo Ren Turn To The Dark Side?

One complaint some people have had about Episode VII is how Kylo Ren almost comes off like a poor man's Darth Vader, right down to the all-black outfit, red lightsaber, and allegiance to an all-powerful user of the Dark Side of the Force. He even wears a voice-distorting mask despite the fact that, unlike Vader, Kylo Ren doesn't need it to survive.

Though there are differences, it is true that Kylo Ren's emulation of Vader is pretty striking, and in fact we discover that Kylo Ren very much tries to pattern himself after his grandfather. While it appears on the surface to be just another case of a Skywalker going down the wrong path, it would be boring to retell the same story we've already seen, so there is obviously going to be more to it than what we saw in Episode VII.

What exactly caused the rift between Ben Solo and his parents? How did Snoke seduce him to the Dark Side, especially in light of the fact that Han, Luke, and Leia would have been extra careful to make sure he didn't wind up like his grandfather? Well, maybe…

He knew he wasn't as powerful as other Force-wielding members of his family, and turned to the Dark Side to prove his worth.

Kylo Ren displayed some amazing talents in Episode VII, such as the ability to freeze blaster bolts in midair and literally read the minds of people under his control. These were things that even Darth Vader couldn't do, and that tells you that Kylo Ren might have even more raw Force power than Vader did.

However, he also displayed some pretty glaring weaknesses that showed he had a long way to go to match his grandfather's skill level. For one, he wasn't close to the warrior that Vader was, as he struggled to defeat Finn on Starkiller Base and then was actually defeated by Rey.

Yes, he was injured after Chewbacca shot him, and yes, both Finn and Rey knew how to take care of themselves even before getting ahold of Luke's lightsaber. Regardless, they still shouldn't have been able to overcome someone who had literally spent years training in the ways of the Force like Kylo Ren had.

Kylo's raw power also failed to overcome the will of someone who had literally just discovered she could use the Force, as we saw when he tried to read Rey's mind to discover Luke Skywalker's location. Not only did he fail to do so, Rey actually turned it around on Kylo and read his mind, learning his true driving force and then using that knowledge to make him lose control by telling him he'd never be as powerful as Darth Vader.

There's also the matter of his lightsaber, which is pretty menacing looking, but amateurish and unstable. Construction of a lightsaber is the mark of one who has mastered the ways of the Force, and the unsteady nature of his lightsaber's beam gives away the fact that Kylo Ren wasn't quite ready for that challenge yet.

It seems pretty likely that Ben Solo regarded his mastery of the Force, or lack thereof, as a measure of his own personal worth. Realizing that he wasn't as strong as he wanted to be, or thought he should be, would have resulted in an overwhelming frustration and embarrassment that left him easy pickings for his new master...

He struggled under Luke Skywalker's guidance, and Snoke showed him a faster path to the power he coveted.

Han and Leia made it pretty clear that they knew their son "had too much Vader in him" as he struggled to manage his use of the

Force. Knowing they weren't equipped to help Ben themselves, they sent him to his uncle, Luke Skywalker, for formal training in the ways of the Force.

As we found out, that didn't turn out too well since Ben fell under the sway of Supreme Leader Snoke, became Kylo Ren, and wiped out Luke's other students in the New Jedi Order. But what happened between the time he left his parents and the time he joined Snoke to cause this drastic change in character?

Regardless of what specific events led to Kylo Ren's betrayal, the end result was that their time together left Kylo without much respect for Uncle Luke. If the main issue was that he didn't progress in his mastery of the Force as quickly as he wanted, he may have blamed that on Luke for not doing (or being able to do) more to get him where he expected to be.

Depending on how much he was around Luke growing up, Ben may have also spent his childhood more familiar with the legend of Luke Skywalker than he was with the man himself. The man who defeated the Sith and destroyed the Empire would cast a pretty large shadow, certainly one that would be difficult to live up to in reality.

Once he actually began to live and train with him, however, he may have been disappointed to discover that Luke wasn't quite what he expected. Possibly expecting Luke to conduct himself as a powerful alpha male type, Ben might have perceived Luke to be weak since Luke wasn't the type to use his power to gain the same ends Ben might have in his place.

That would be where Snoke comes in. Dark Side types tend to be a lot more power hungry and self-indulgent than the Jedi, and definitely weren't shy about showing how powerful they were.

The chance to gain the kind of power that Snoke would

have been so cavalier about showing off would be tough for a young Force user with self-esteem issues to resist. If Snoke promised to make Ben far more powerful than Luke ever could, there wouldn't be much of an internal debate in Ben's head before deciding to take Snoke up on his offer.

He idolized his grandfather, Darth Vader.

While this was made pretty clear during the movie, there might have been more to it than simply the mastery of the Force that Ben so desperately craved. As we saw, Kylo Ren had recovered the helmet and skull of his grandfather, Darth Vader, and used it as a sort of idol to guide him through his journey to the Dark Side.

It's important to point out that Kylo Ren's hero-worship is for Darth Vader, and not Anakin Skywalker. He ignores the fact that Anakin redeemed himself by killing Palpatine shortly before his death, and has apparently cast Anakin off with the rest of his family and regards Darth Vader as his "true" grandfather.

The fact that Kylo Ren is so loyal to the legend of Darth Vader (again, relying on the stories that make Vader out to be ten feet tall since he never met the man himself) that he actually went to Endor to retrieve his remains says a lot. While he clearly did not hold Luke in high regard, Kylo Ren has put Vader on a pedestal as the standard he wants to mold himself in the image of.

Darth Vader was obviously one of the most powerful warriors and practitioners of the Force to ever live, but he also wielded incredible political power, second only to the Emperor himself. People feared Vader not just for his own deadly strength, but also because he had the entire might of the Empire backing him up.

Aside from offering to complete his Force training, Snoke also gave Kylo Ren the same position in the First Order that

Vader held in the Empire. Well, almost: he is constantly at odds with Captain Phasma and General Hux, who have formed a sort of command triumverate who all report to Snoke, but otherwise have equal power to one another.

Knowing that Kylo Ren desires to emulate Vader above all else, Snoke put him in a position where he is forced to compete with Hux and Phasma to gain and keep his favor. Having already come up short in his prior Force training under Luke, Kylo Ren would be terrified of failing Snoke and losing his place at his new master's side, and will do anything to prevent that.

Snoke obviously knows how to manipulate Kylo Ren to his ends, and uses this arrangement to keep Kylo on a pretty short leash. In fact, he might have even used Kylo Ren's Vader-worship to manipulate him in another way...

Snoke drove a wedge of distrust between Ben and his family.

Turning Kylo Ren against Luke Skywalker would be a given considering the threat Luke would be to Snoke's plans for conquest. We saw earlier how Snoke might have gone about turning Ben Solo against his uncle, but why the malice toward his parents?

Sure, they were the ones who sent him to Luke in the first place, but does that really warrant a desire for Kylo Ren to kill his own father like he did? Possibly, if Snoke drew upon Vader's past to set Kylo's path in this regard.

For one, Snoke could point to the fact that Kylo's parents and uncle were three of the key players in the Rebellion that ultimately destroyed Darth Vader and his Empire, and use that to poison him against his own family.

Obi-Wan Kenobi and Yoda vilified Emperor Palpatine and Darth Vader for bringing an end to the Republic, and that point of view greatly influenced Luke's choice of path in the original trilogy. Snoke could have done the same with Kylo Ren, only portraying his own family as the villains for bringing about the "dark times" by destroying the Empire.

Snoke could have also used the manner of Vader's death to his advantage. Yoda told Luke that he needed to face and defeat his father before he could become a Jedi himself. Knowing this, Snoke likely told Kylo he needed to do the same to take the next step toward the power he coveted.

Despite the anger he had for his family, Kylo obviously struggled with the task that lay before him. He even came right out and told Han that there was something he had to do, but wasn't sure if he had the strength to do it.

Han was more than happy to help his son, not realizing that Kylo meant to kill him. He obviously found out soon enough, but the fact that Kylo was willing to cross that line on Snoke's word alone showed what a masterful job the mysterious Supreme Leader had done subverting him to his cause.

However, the fact that Snoke knows enough of this history to manipulate Kylo Ren with it is interesting in and of itself. He seems to know more about the events of the original trilogy than anyone who wasn't involved should, so that begs the question...

Who Is Supreme Leader Snoke?

Kylo Ren and Darth Vader had more in common than a shared family line, Force powers, and a red lightsaber. They also both answered to evil, shadowy beings who operated in secrecy while letting their enforcers do their dirty work for them. Vader was the right hand man of the Sith Lord Palpatine, while Kylo Ren follows the lead of Snoke, the mysterious Supreme Leader of the First Order.

We know very little about Supreme Leader Snoke at this stage of the game since he was far away from the action in Episode VII. Where did he come from? What is his motivation in creating the First Order? What are his true goals that even his followers don't know?

It may be a while before we know the answers to all of those questions, but we can hazard a few guesses as to his origin, such as...

He is a secret apprentice of Emperor Palpatine.

Even though the Sith had the Rule of Two, which stated that there could only ever be two Sith at any given time, Palpatine would have probably had no problem defying the rule to serve his own needs. In fact, he already had at least once before.

Despite the fact that he was still the apprentice of Darth Plagueis at the time, Palpatine raised Darth Maul from the time he was a baby and trained him in the ways of the Force in direct defiance of the Rule of Two. Though this was never touched on in the movie, Darth Plagueis was actually still alive when Episode I began, and was murdered by Palpatine the night before he was elected Supreme Chancellor of the Republic.

Given his willingness to go against the rules of the Sith

Order when it suited him, it's not a stretch to suggest that Palpatine secretly trained other apprentices that even Darth Vader wasn't aware of. Remember, Palpatine didn't even appear in person in the original trilogy until he arrived on the Second Death Star, so we have no idea what he was doing and with who the rest of the time.

If Snoke was another apprentice of Palpatine's who managed to stay out of sight when the Empire fell, his motivation for wanting to destroy the Jedi and re-establish Imperial rule, albeit in a different form, would be pretty obvious. It would also explain his obsession with hunting down Luke Skywalker: to avenge his master's death.

He is a reincarnation of Emperor Palpatine.

Nobody in Star Wars had the same kind of foresight as Emperor Palpatine, not even Yoda. Given that, it's hard to imagine that he wouldn't have made some kind of preparations for the possibility of his own death, however unlikely it might have seemed at any given point.

Palpatine had already changed the dynamic of the Sith Order once when he violated the Rule of Two. It wouldn't be surprising to find out that Palpatine never intended to be replaced by Darth Vader according to Sith custom, either, and had a plan to stick around even in the event of his demise.

Palpatine was obsessed with his quest for power, and like most such power-hungry tyrants, he would have also been obsessed with not losing that power once he had it. He spoke to Anakin about his master's ability to prevent death, so what if Palpatine eventually discovered the secret to that very skill himself?

If Palpatine had discovered the secret to immortality, there's exactly one person he would ever use it for, and that's himself. Yoda may not have been strong enough with the Force to prevent his own death, but Palpatine may have been if he managed to replicate his master's success. If he had, he could have had the foresight to use the skill as a backup plan in case he met an unexpected end.

That backup plan may have been reincarnation as Supreme Leader Snoke. Like Palpatine, Snoke is a charismatic leader who created a highly powerful and loyal military force, masterminded the creation of a world-destroying weapon, and has lured a powerful, Force-wielding Skywalker to the Dark Side.

There's a lot of similarities there, but we also have to consider another Sith Lord whom we've heard a bit about, but have yet to meet...

He is the reincarnation of Darth Plagueis.

Pretty much all we know about Darth Plagueis is that he was Palpatine's Sith Master, and he had developed the ability to create and preserve life through manipulation of the Force. Once again, wouldn't the first thing any Sith Lord did once attaining such a power be to ensure the preservation of his own life?

You can't be a Sith Lord and be a dummy. Darth Plagueis would have recognized Palpatine's true character long before he was murdered by his apprentice. After all, Sith apprentices murdering their masters to take control of the Order had been the way of the Sith for thousands of years, so Plagueis would have been expecting Palpatine to try and kill him eventually.

If Plagueis' ability to manipulate life and death was as strong as Palpatine made it out to be, there's a chance that he could have survived without his former apprentice being any the wiser. If he had, Plagueis could have remained hidden until Palpatine was gone so he could once more emerge unchallenged as the undisputed Sith Master.

Given that Plagueis was the one who originally formulated the plan leading to Palpatine's rise to power, everything Snoke has done to build his power in the years prior to Episode VII could simply be the resumption of his work prior to the death of his former self.

He is a former Jedi who survived the Purge.

Even though they were the only ones who continued actively working to defeat the Sith, we never knew for sure whether Yoda and Obi-Wan Kenobi were really the only Jedi to survive the Jedi Purge in Episode III. Remember, they did transmit out a warning to let any other surviving Jedi know what had happened, so if some lucky stragglers did receive that message before the Clone Army found them, then they could have survived and gone into hiding as Yoda and Obi-Wan eventually did.

Any other surviving Jedi would have done one of two things: either try (and inevitably fail) to stop the Sith themselves, or spend the next twenty years hiding out from the Sith who had taken over the galaxy. Once the Empire was destroyed, however, the Jedi who had remained in hiding may have become a little braver about showing their faces, and may have even had ideas about rebuilding the Jedi Order.

After spending so many years with little to do other than mull over how things had turned out the way they had, the surviving Jedi may have come to the conclusion that the Jedi Order was simply too passive about hunting down the Sith. Believing that the Jedi had gotten too soft in the years leading up to their near-extinction, the survivors may have decided that the New Jedi Order would need a more aggressive edge to prevent a repeat of what had happened before.

As they began working to rebuild the Jedi Order, however, the surviving Jedi would have discovered that someone else claiming to be not just a Jedi Master, but the son of the very man who had destroyed the Jedi in the first place, was already rebuilding the Jedi Order in his own vision.

Considering themselves the rightful heirs to the Jedi legacy, and regarding Luke Skywalker as an unworthy and dangerous fraud, the older and more seasoned Jedi would in no way stand for anyone named Skywalker trying to hijack the Jedi Order again. They would do whatever they must to prevent Luke from subverting the Order with the same weak-minded philosophy that had destroyed it the first time.

If Snoke was an original Jedi who wanted to create a new version of the Jedi Order that lived by a harder-edged philosophy, then Luke Skywalker would be the biggest obstacle toward attaining that goal. Perhaps the reason Snoke took Kylo Ren was to mold him into his vision of what the "new" Jedi should be, and use him as an example that Luke Skywalker wouldn't be able to ignore.

He is a Force-sensitive being with no formal group affiliation.

Then again, there's also the possibility that Snoke doesn't have any connection to anyone we've met in the past, and is just a brand new character with an unknown background. Anakin Skywalker was apparently conceived by the Force, so what's to say that he was the only instance of the Force manifesting itself in this way?

If Snoke is another such being and wields as much power as Anakin Skywalker did, that would make him a major threat to Luke Skywalker and anyone else standing in his way. The fact that he specifically targeted Han and Leia's son to subvert to the Dark Side would suggest that he at least knows the history of the war between the Jedi and the Sith, and has figured out how to use it to his advantage as he continues to build the power of the First Order.

Who Are The Knights Of Ren?

Though we were briefly introduced to the Knights of Ren during Rey's vision sequence on Takodana, we know very, very little about them at this point in time. We know Kylo Ren is their master, that there are at least six more of them, and that they answer to Supreme Leader Snoke.

Other than that, we learned nothing about who the Knights of Ren are or what they were doing while Episode VII was happening. We'll probably need to wait until at least Episode VIII to find out more about them, but here are some possible backstories...

They are the spiritual successors to the Sith.

Even though the Sith themselves died with Darth Vader and Emperor Palpatine, it's obvious that the Dark Side is still alive and well when the events of Episode VII roll around. We know for sure that Snoke and Kylo Ren are practitioners of the Dark Side, and it wouldn't be surprising to discover that the Knights of Ren are as well.

One thing that is clear about the Knights of Ren is that they are firmly on the anti-Jedi side of things. Rey's vision would seem to indicate that they were with Kylo Ren when he began to wipe out Luke's other trainees, and since their master wants to embrace the Dark Side so badly that he actually begged Darth Vader's skull to show him the way, we can see a very deliberate attempt to continue operating in the spirit of the Sith philosophy.

How far the similarities between the Sith and the Knights of Ren go is something we're going to have to wait to see, but right off the bat, we know the Rule of Two is no longer in effect. Between Snoke, Kylo Ren, and the rest of the bunch, we've got eight right there, and there may be more who didn't tag along for Kylo's Jedi killing spree.

73

Also unlike the Sith, the Knights of Ren are very much okay with operating in plain view. Though the Sith policy on secrecy may have changed once the Emperor came to power and the Jedi were thought wiped out, the Sith spent centuries operating in the shadows to avoid discovery and destruction at the hands of the Jedi. They also picked their spots very carefully, preferring subterfuge to slugging it out with the Jedi on a level playing field.

The Knights of Ren showed no such considerations, even with Luke Skywalker leading the New Jedi Order, and mounted a direct (and successful) attack on the Jedi. That's not a move I could ever envision Palpatine making, but if Kylo Ren is typical of the other members, then the Knights of Ren are much younger than the average Sith was, and therefore may be more prone to taking those sorts of uncalculated risks.

They are a group created by Snoke for the sole purpose of subverting Ben Solo to the Dark Side.

Going back to the idea that Snoke gave Kylo Ren the same spot in the First Order that Darth Vader occupied in the Empire as a way of validating his ego to make him easier to control, Snoke may have also created the Knights of Ren just to give Kylo Ren an elite commission in a secret society similar to Vader's role in the Sith Order.

That seems like a lot of trouble to go through just to try and get a young, poorly-trained kid under contract, so to speak, but it's not without precedent in the real world. Many times, entire new job titles are created by companies simply to satisfy disgruntled, but valuable employees they'd rather not see go elsewhere.

Another good analogy is the "everybody gets a trophy" phenomenon seen in recent years, at least in the United States. For those unfamiliar with this, it's a system whereby everyone on the team gets "participation trophies" regardless of whether they win the league or suffer crushing losses every time they take the field.

You can definitely see a spoiled sense of entitlement in Kylo Ren's personality, as well as a belief that he should be more than he is simply based on his heritage. As simplistic as it sounds, the Knights of Ren could just be a fancy participation trophy that only exists for Kylo Ren's sake.

Kylo Ren wouldn't ever need to know that Snoke had literally created the Knights of Ren out of thin air, and it also wouldn't matter if the rest of the group were a bunch of incompetent ringers. In fact, they might serve Snoke's purposes even better if they're demonstrably less spectacular than Kylo Ren, since that would just serve to pump up Kylo Ren's ego even more.

Bottom line: as long as Kylo Ren felt like he was evolving into the same kind of figure his grandfather was, and being patted on the head and assured he's a superstar whether or not his skills or accomplishments actually measure up, he'd be getting what he wanted.

They were created by Kylo Ren as his own personal anti-Jedi squad.

While it's not unheard of for someone without use of the Force to take down someone who does, wiping out an entire group of Jedi trainees would seem like a pretty tall order for non-Force users to take on. Kylo Ren may not respect Luke Skywalker's power, but he still wouldn't be dumb enough to show up to fight him with just a mob of rent-a-thugs.

No, Kylo Ren would know he'd need to bring some serious muscle to overcome his former master and his apprentices. To that end, he may have created the Knights of Ren (or been guided to do so by Snoke) specifically to destroy Luke and the Jedi.

So where did he get the others? Well, he could have trained them all himself, but as we've seen, his skills aren't quite up to the heavyweight division just yet. It's not likely that he had the ability (or the patience, for that matter) to train others, so they were probably already trained when they joined the group.

What if they were other Jedi apprentices that followed Ben Solo when he split with Luke and sided with Snoke? It's never been explicitly stated that he killed each and every one of Luke's other trainees, so it's possible that some of them joined Ben as charter members of the Knights of Ren.

Of course, it is possible that none of them can use the Force, or at least are novices who are unable to use it to any great effect. The fact that Kylo Ren is the master of the Knights of Ren would suggest that he is the most powerful of the bunch, and he was also the only one we saw brandishing a lightsaber during Rey's vision.

While that doesn't necessarily mean the others can't use the Force, they may still not be far enough in their own training to even make a novice attempt at constructing a lightsaber like Kylo Ren did. If Kylo created the group himself, odds are that they're nowhere near as threatening, at least individually, as their leader.

Of course, if their original leader was a certain someone else, that might change things...

They are a secret group created and trained by Darth Vader.

We already know that Palpatine was willing to disregard the Rule of Two by training Darth Maul while still apprenticed to Darth Plagueis, and also speculated on the possibility that Snoke was another apprentice of his that even Darth Vader knew nothing about.

However, what if Vader took a page out of the Emperor's book by training secret apprentices of his own? The goal of every Sith apprentice is to eventually kill their master and take control of the Sith Order for themselves, so what if Vader prepared for this eventuality by training apprentices in the ways of the Sith to assist him when the confrontation with Palpatine eventually happened?

As powerful as Vader was, he would have known that Palpatine was no pushover since he had fought both Mace Windu and Yoda and lived to tell the tale. What's more, Palpatine's Sith lightning would (and eventually did) kill Vader by destroying his life support suit, so if he were ever to take a shot at Palpatine, he probably wouldn't be able to do it alone.

One way Vader might have approached a war with his master would be to train his own group of Sith to act as his proxies and fight Palpatine in his place, possibly with Vader using the Force to support them from a distance. It may still have not worked, but Vader may have thought it sounded like as good a plan as any.

If that was Vader's intent, then he would have never had the chance to put it into action since he and the Emperor were both killed on the Second Death Star. This would have left the Knights of Ren, Sith in practice if not in name, without a leader or a purpose.

As a powerful user of the Dark Side of the Force, Snoke could have discovered them and brought them under his wing. Once he discovered that the drive to recreate himself in his grandfather's image was Ben Solo's Achilles heel, it would have been a natural fit to play into that by making him the leader of the very same group that Vader founded.

They existed at the time Kylo Ren betrayed Luke Skywalker, but have since ceased to exist.

Of course, we may not have seen the other Knights of Ren in Episode VII because they had all been killed or otherwise left the group since the events from Rey's vision took place.

That could have happened through any of a dozen different scenarios, but just because Snoke referred to Kylo as the master of the Knights of Ren doesn't mean he currently has other Knights of Ren to lead. Kylo would still officially hold that title, but the group itself could have a membership of one at the time Episode VII happened.

Why Has Leia Still Not Learned To Use The Force?

Luke, Obi-Wan, and Yoda all believed that Leia had inherited enough of Anakin Skywalker's strength with the Force that she could be their backup plan should Luke fail in his quest to destroy the Empire. Luckily for Leia, Luke came through in the end and she never ended up having to put her Force powers to the test.

In the thirty years since the fall of the Empire, however, Leia didn't appear to have made any effort to try and realize the potential of her power. She was obviously Force-sensitive enough to sense Han's death, but beyond that, she hadn't made any apparent headway in all the years since she learned her true origins.

It seems like a no-brainer to want to explore the ways of the Force if you know you're able to, so why was Leia still sitting at headquarters like she always had while everyone else was out there dodging blaster rays? It could be because...

She decided to focus on her family instead.

Now that we know for sure that Han and Leia stayed together and had a family, as many people long assumed they would after the events of Return of the Jedi, Leia could have been so focused on Han and her young son that she simply didn't have the time to think about the Force or Jedi training.

If this is what happened, then Leia's decision to trade in her family birthright for a soccer mom minivan had backfired by the time her son Ben began to show definite signs of being able to use the Force. Knowing that she wasn't equipped to guide her son through the unique adolescence he was about to experience, she sent Ben to train with his Uncle Luke, and as we saw, that arrangement eventually fell apart in violent fashion.

Leia and Han had an interesting conversation when they reunited, as Han said he didn't think he could get through to his son if Luke couldn't, but Leia was adamant that, while Luke was a Jedi Master, Han was Ben's father. Though that didn't end up making much of a difference when it came down to it, if Leia had chosen to take up her power, she could have averted Ben's fall to the Dark Side as both a parent AND a Force mentor.

She made a conscious choice to distance herself from the Skywalker legacy.

Could Leia have chosen not to explore her power because, despite the revelation of who her father was, she still didn't identify herself as a Skywalker? Her lack of a visible reaction when Luke told her who she really was seemed strange at the time, but it's possible it could have just been that it didn't change anything about who she saw herself as.

Unlike Luke, who was raised by Owen and Beru out of an apparent feeling of obligation, Senator Bail Organa genuinely wanted Leia to be a part of his family. While Luke was helping scrape out a lowly living on a desert planet, Leia lived in comfort in a palace on Alderaan, and eventually became a member of the Imperial Senate in her own right.

It's not at all uncommon for adopted children to consider the family who took them in as their "real" parents, even if the biological parents eventually come back into the picture. While she may have been surprised to find out who her biological father was, she may not have been too rattled by it because she still thought of Bail Organa as her father, not Anakin Skywalker or Darth Vader.

Unlike Luke, who grew up with some knowledge of his real father, Leia likely never knew anything and probably didn't dwell on it to any great degree. While Luke yearned for a life of meaning off of Tatooine, Leia already had one as an Organa, and the idea of foregoing all of that to acknowledge herself as the daughter of someone she regarded as an evil tyrant may not have been an appealing one.

Even though Vader was long gone by the time Episode VII happened, she still wasn't using the Skywalker name and still referred to herself as Leia Organa. In addition to never using her real last name, an intentional decision to not embrace the Skywalker legacy may have also caused her to reject the idea of learning the ways of the Force, especially after seeing what it had done to Ben.

She tried, but turned out not to be that strong with the Force after all.

During the original trilogy, the main clues we got that Leia was in touch with the Force were when she sensed that Luke was in trouble after his fight with Darth Vader on Cloud City, and again when she sensed he was alive after the destruction of the Second Death Star. Then, in Episode VII, she sensed Han's death the moment it happened.

However, sensing whether those close to her are dead or not could be the extent of her Force powers. Though this might be a bit of a simplistic way of looking at it, the same way a father being a superstar at a sport doesn't necessarily mean the kids will be, Anakin Skywalker's affinity with the Force might not necessarily pass down equally to both his children.

In that regard, Luke might have been the chip off the old block who showed an aptitude at a young age and eventually followed his dad to a championship NFL career. Leia, on the other hand, could have been the one who tried it because everyone else in her family did, but wasn't very good and gave up after two years on the varsity squad.

Thirty years would have given Leia plenty of time to train with Luke if she had wanted, but if she didn't have the ability to do the things Luke could, or if her...difficult personality interfered with her training (possibly explaining how the same thing could have happened with Ben), then she might have decided not to waste her time after all.

She has, and we just haven't found out yet.

Even though she was in Episode VII, Leia mostly hung out at Resistance headquarters, and didn't really see any action other than tagging along with the Resistance force that showed up on Takodana. While Leia was always a lot more comfortable hiding out in command centers than putting herself in the line of fire, the fact is that she didn't get put into a position where she would have had to use whatever Force powers she might have.

One would think that if Leia did have use of the Force beyond the little we've seen, she would have used it when her son began displaying his Vader-like tendencies. At the very least, she would have tried to help guide him herself before sending him off to Luke. We may see her pull out some tricks in Episode VIII or IX, but I wouldn't hold my breath.

What Is Finn's True Background?

Unlike the clone soldiers who served as the initial basis for the Imperial Army, Finn revealed that the Stormtroopers who served the First Order were taken from their families at a young age and programmed to perform the duties and functions their masters desired.

Finn eventually grew disenchanted with the system and escaped. He later revealed to Rey that he had so little information about his previous life that he didn't even know his real name or where he was originally from.

Mysterious origins of major characters are never brought up in movies unless there's a plan to reveal the truth somewhere down the line. It's more than likely that, at some point, we'll find out everything we ever wanted to know about Finn's origins.

For now though, all we really know about him is what the First Order let him know. There's a few different ways they could go with this, so let's talk about what we might discover when we finally learn Finn's true identity…

Finn was just a normal kid from an unremarkable family and humble surroundings.

This is what the situation would appear to be at first glance, given what Finn himself had to say about his background. To hear him tell it, the bulk of the First Order army is made up of children who had been kidnapped from their families before they were old enough to have any awareness of where or even who they were.

Their true identities cease to exist at that point, and they become little more than assets owned by their new masters. They're given an impersonal identification number, raised to obey the ideals and expectations of the First Order, and otherwise treated as little more than mindless robots.

Finn said he was so young when he was taken that he doesn't remember anything about his real family, or even what his birth name was. His family history is a complete blank in his mind, and there are some very good reasons an organization like the First Order would want it that way.

The First Order wants a completely loyal army, one that will blindly follow orders without any potential for conflicting allegiances. Prior attachments to people or places with personal significance can become liabilities on the battlefield, and the First Order would rather not have these complications arise at an inconvenient moment.

This system of kidnapping children and forcing them into military service has happened many times throughout history in real life, and the armies who take them have usually done it for two reasons.

One is to make sure the soldiers would destroy their own homes without a second thought if they were ordered to. Since they don't know where they're originally from, this shouldn't be an issue.

The other reason is to make sure the places they attack are reluctant to defend themselves if it means killing their own children. Finn may have no idea who he is, but if the First Order were to attack his home planet, his parents might recognize him when he came rushing in with guns blazing.

Rather than risk harming their children, however corrupted they've become, the defenders may instead choose to lay down their arms, or at least offer minimal resistance while the First Order's forces mowed them down.

Finn is the son of Lando Calrissian.

Lando Calrissian was conspicuously absent from Episode VII, neither appearing nor having his name brought up even in passing. It seems strange to leave someone of his stature out of the story given how important he was to the Rebel victory thirty years earlier, yet he was nowhere to be found.

But what if Lando was intentionally left out of the picture for the time being because he will return later on, albeit for a reason that has nothing to do with the Rebellion? What if, like it already has for the Skywalker/Solo family, the sequel trilogy becomes a Calrissian family affair?

The theory that Finn will turn out to be Lando's son is one of the most popular currently making the rounds. The fact that Lando was one of the only significant black characters in the previous chapters probably has something to do with that, but there are other reasons this theory might hold some water.

For one, Snoke obviously has a very detailed knowledge of the key players involved in the wars between the Rebellion and the Empire. Even if he wasn't currently involved in the conflict himself, Lando would be known to Snoke, and the Supreme Leader would already have a way of manipulating him worked out in his playbook.

We've also seen that Snoke has shown a willingness to hit his enemies close to home by using their children as pawns, such he has with Kylo Ren. What if Finn was kidnapped as a child so he could be used as blackmail in case Lando ever got any ideas about getting involved?

Then again, Finn could be Lando's son and nobody realizes it, not even Lando! Given the lifestyle Lando led prior to getting involved with the Rebellion (and possibly after, as well), would it be a surprise to find out he fathered an illegitimate child he never found out about?

Sure, that wouldn't be particularly useful to the First Order, or to Finn or Lando, for that matter. But if Finn is Lando's son, legitimate or not, it would be a great way of reintroducing someone who should have been in Episode VII, but wasn't.

Finn's family was somehow aligned with the Dark Side.

Sometimes, when a person with no knowledge of their past finally finds out the truth, they don't always like what they discover. This could turn out to be the case if we come to learn that Finn's parents are practitioners of the Dark Side of the Force.

This would explain how, at times, Finn showed glimmers of Force sensitivity during his voyage with Rey, Han, and Chewbacca. Having parents in touch with the Force, albeit the Dark Side, would make Finn likely to inherit similar powers, as we've already seen in the Skywalker family.

That said, anyone with use of the Dark Side probably wouldn't just stand there and let Snoke waltz in and take their kid. They might be willing to work something out, but outright kidnapping would probably turn things uglier than Snoke would want them to get.

After all, wouldn't Snoke prefer to have fellow Dark Side adepts on his side instead of making enemies out of them at the same time he's trying to fight the Jedi? Is even he powerful enough to fight a two-front war like that?

I find it hard to believe Snoke would be dumb enough to pick more fights than he could handle at any given point. More likely, he would prefer to find a way to handle the situation diplomatically...at least for the time being.

That raises the possibility that instead, of being forcibly

taken, Finn's parents willingly gave him up to Snoke to further the Dark Side agenda. How would Finn react if he discovered that, instead of longing for the return of their lost son, his parents had literally sold him down the river?

Rather than the hapless weaklings we might imagine them as, Finn's parents could have been among Snoke's First Order officers, possibly even on Starkiller Base. Finn could have emptied their garbage pails every day for all he knew, and never once realized who they really were.

Finn never had a family because he is an artificially created life form.

During one of their series of backhanded exchanges after Rey and Finn escaped Jakku with BB-8, Kylo Ren blamed General Hux's army for letting them slip through, and suggested that they might get better results with clone soldiers instead.

General Hux was obviously insulted by the insinuation that his highly-trained, elite military was not on the level of an army of manufactured drones. However, what if Hux already had a clone soldier in his forces and didn't even realize it?

The original Imperial Army was, of course, made up entirely of clones of the bounty hunter, Jango Fett. They were all sentient, fully functional beings who had been programmed from the beginning to wage war, but they didn't have "parents" in the traditional sense.

Along the same lines, what if Finn can't remember his family because he never had one to begin with? What if he were himself an artificial being, possibly a prototype for a new breed of clone soldier, and even General Hux himself didn't know?

This drifts further toward the realm of possibility when you consider how much focus there was on the fact that FN-2187 (as he was known to the First Order) scored very high in all their target metrics before going off the reservation and defecting to the Resistance. The confusion almost made it seem as if he were an experiment gone wrong.

But what if he wasn't? If Finn really is an artificial being, what if he decided to defect to the Resistance because he was intentionally programmed to do so? Could he be be a sleeper cell the First Order planted behind enemy lines to attack from within once activated?

Finn might not even realize what his true purpose would be if this is the case, especially if his secret orders were biologically imprinted in him the way Order 66 was in the Clone Army. If Finn does turn out to be a Manchurian Candidate, then he might not be the only one surprised to find out the truth.

Why Did Luke Skywalker Disappear?

The first thing we learned as Episode VII began was that the Jedi Master who had toppled the Sith and destroyed the First Galactic Empire had vanished. The entire movie revolved around the effort to find Luke, and even though Rey finally tracked him down at the end of the movie, we left off before finding out what exactly caused him to leave in the first place.

Han Solo gave Rey and Finn a couple of theories when he first ran into them on the Millennium Falcon, but even he didn't seem to know for sure. Why would a powerful Jedi Master like Luke Skywalker, who had already defeated the most powerful adversaries the Jedi ever faced, suddenly pull a disappearing act when such a dangerous threat as Snoke and the First Order popped up?

Let's explore Han's ideas, and also see what else we can come up with on our own...

He felt responsible for Snoke's rise to power, and removed himself to avoid making things worse than they already were.

When Return of the Jedi ended, Luke had brought about the fall of the Galactic Empire, the destruction of the Second Death Star, the death of Emperor Palpatine, the redemption of Anakin Skywalker, and the demise of the Sith Order that had survived in secret for a thousand years. He had become the Grand Master of the Jedi, and looked forward to a bright future spent rebuilding the Jedi Order and a new Galactic Republic.

Thirty years later, the New Republic is in danger of being completely annihilated by a military junta born out of the remains of the Empire he had destroyed, a mysterious, Force-wielding monster has seduced his nephew to the Dark Side, and that same nephew thwarted his attempts to resurrect the Jedi Order by wiping out his other students.

You can understand how this sequence of events would be discouraging to Luke, because not only has the galaxy essentially wound up back at square one, but his own nephew, whom Luke himself trained in the ways of the Force, became one of the key players in putting it there. Feeling at the very least that he had accomplished nothing, and at worst that things might not have gotten so bad if he hadn't trained Ben to begin with, Luke may very well have decided that the best thing he could do for the galaxy would be to just stay out of the way.

He went looking for the First Jedi Temple.

Then again, I think most of us would expect Luke to show a little more heart and determination than that. This is the guy who, after all, was ready to throw his life away on multiple occasions if there was even a chance it would help his friends or defeat the Emperor. What are the odds that he'd let something like this beat him after all he'd been through?

Han mentioned that, in the wake of Ben's transformation into Kylo Ren, Luke might have left to go looking for the First Jedi Temple. If Snoke turns out to be as powerful as earlier Dark Side practitioners like Palpatine or Vader, then Luke may have realized that he was up against an opponent he couldn't beat on his own.

Rather than hiding out of fear for his life, Luke may have made a strategic decision to disengage for the time being and search for something that would give him an edge against Snoke. With the Jedi Temple on Coruscant long since sacked by the Sith, the First Jedi Temple would have seemed like the next best place to go searching for a way to defeat this new threat.

Ancient temples like that are often where heroes in these kinds of stories find some kind of ultimate power that has been locked away for centuries. These ultimate weapons have usually been hidden since even their owners are afraid of their sheer power, and being the conscientious bunch they were, that's exactly what the Jedi would have done if they feared it could be misused.

Since things are looking pretty bleak by the time Episode VII starts, there's a good chance that Luke discovered whatever this ultimate power is and decided that now's the time to use it.

He went into hiding to commune with the spirits of dead Jedi.

As we saw many times during the original trilogy, Luke was visited by the spirits of Obi-Wan Kenobi and, later, Yoda and Anakin. Luke's mentors had always been there to help guide him through his darkest moments, and given how hopeless Luke's situation seemed after Snoke came to power, he may have turned to them for guidance once more.

This is, of course, assuming that Luke had the ability to summon the spirits of his dead mentors on his own, and didn't need to rely on their willingness or ability to reach out to him themselves. Obi-Wan and Yoda may have been able to stick around because of their will to see the destruction of the Sith through to completion, but now that their task has been completed, their spirits have finally gone to rest.

Then again, this might not be such a huge hurdle for Luke to get over, either. Before going into exile at the end of Episode III, Yoda informed Obi-Wan that he had a final lesson for him. Using the knowledge imparted by Yoda, Obi-Wan spent his exile on Tatooine learning to commune with the spirits of dead Jedi, including his old master, Qui Gon Jinn.

It's not known whether Yoda or Obi-Wan taught Luke this skill, or if he figured it out on his own in the years after the fall of the

Empire (or maybe even discovered the technique at the First Jedi Temple). If he did, however, it would have opened him up to a world of wisdom far beyond what Yoda, Anakin, and Obi-Wan, as wise and powerful as they were, could teach him on their own.

The ability to commune with dead Jedi would open him up to the minds of literally thousands of spirits who had served the Jedi Order in life, faced countless terrors and evil menaces, and conquered seemingly insurmountable odds. Even if he was stuck for a plan on how to deal with Snoke, the guidance of every Jedi who had ever lived would make a great starting point.

Luke suspected he wouldn't be around much longer, and wanted to make preparations for others to take up the Jedi cause after he was gone.

After the fall of the Jedi, Yoda and Obi-Wan Kenobi knew they would never again be able to challenge the Sith themselves. Instead, they focused the last twenty years or so of their lives laying the groundwork for their successors, specifically Anakin's children, to take up the Jedi mantle and hopefully defeat the Sith in their stead.

Luke, who is around the same age in Episode VII as Obi-Wan was when everything started breaking down in the original movie, may be of a similar mindset. If Luke is able to admit to himself that he's past his physical prime and possibly not up to taking on Snoke and Kylo Ren by himself, he may have spent the time since his disappearance ensuring that the Jedi Order and everything he had done to preserve and rebuild it wouldn't be lost if he were to die.

There's a pretty good chance Obi-Wan knew that, when he and Luke set off from Tatooine with those droids, he wouldn't be coming back alive. Similarly, Luke could have realized (or divined through the Force) that his next run at Snoke could be a suicide mission. Even if he survived, he'd still be old enough that he probably wouldn't have enough time to properly restore the Jedi Order like he had planned.

With all that being the case, it would make sense if Luke spent the years prior to Episode VII getting everything ready for the next generation of Jedi to take over for him. Luke knows how difficult it is to self-train in the Jedi arts, so if he wasn't expecting to make it back from a battle with Snoke, he'd want to make sure his successors would be as prepared as he could make them without being there to train them himself.

Bonus Features

Have You Seen Me? The People Who Should Have Been In Episode VII (But Weren't)

Luke, Leia, Han, Chewie, C-3PO, and R2-D2 weren't the only characters from the original trilogy to survive the war with the Empire. For some reason, though, many of their most notable surviving friends (and enemies) were nowhere to be found in Episode VII.

In much the same way as the back of milk cartons strive to locate the long-lost, we're going to take a look at the most conspicuous absentees, and see if we can hazard some guesses as to where they've been hiding out while Han and Chewie are once again putting themselves squarely in the line of fire...

Lando Calrissian

Once the administrator of the Cloud City mining facility on Bespin, events soon spiraled out of control and led to him abandoning his post to join the Rebellion. Eventually becoming a General in the Rebel forces, he led the assault on the Second Death Star and fired the shot that destroyed the gigantic battle station from the inside out.

Despite being front and center at the Rebel victory celebration on Endor, Lando's life seemed to take him in a different direction than his friends in the years that followed. He did not rejoin them as they took up the battle against the First Order, and was not on hand for what turned out to be his old friend Han Solo's final mission.

This isn't particularly surprising, knowing his history as a suave, smooth-talking playboy who preferred living in comfort far, far away from conflicts of any kind. Wherever Lando was, odds are it had plenty of booze, gambling, and women...lots and lots of women.

The Ewoks

The unlikeliest of the Rebel allies also turned out to be possibly the most important, as they defeated the Imperial Army on their home planet of Endor and allowed the Rebels to destroy the shield generator protecting the Second Death Star.

The Rebellion would have been finished right then and there if it weren't for the Ewoks. However, much like the natives of Third World nations who are far removed from the media and social peculiarities of what we consider civilization, the Ewoks probably had little grasp of the galactic civilization they had played such a huge part in shaping.

It's hard to imagine the Ewoks having any interest in the lifestyle of the strange people who had passed through their habitat. Not only would they have probably had no interest in taking a bigger part in the New Republic, they were probably happy to see everyone go after all the death and destruction they caused.

Life probably went back to normal for the Ewoks soon after the Rebellion and Empire cleared out. Other than Kylo Ren possibly skewering a few when he stopped by to pick up his grandfather's head, the Ewoks probably never came into contact with anyone not from Endor ever again.

Wedge Antilles

Last seen celebrating the Rebel victory in the Ewok Village, Wedge is probably the most important ancillary character in the entire series. Despite being the kind of background character that usually gets dusted midway through the story to almost no reaction, Wedge survived some of the most hard-fought battles of the war to become perhaps its least-celebrated hero.

Despite surviving the attacks on both Death Stars as well as the defense of the Rebel base on Hoth, Wedge was nowhere to be found thirty years later. Did he get elected to the new Galactic Senate? Did he wind up continuing to serve Leia in the Resistance? Does he host an obscure talk show on a public access channel at the top of the dial? We may never know...even though nobody probably cared all that much to begin with.

Yoda, Obi-Wan Kenobi, and Anakin Skywalker

Obi-Wan Kenobi seemed to appear to Luke in spectral form pretty much at will after being killed by Darth Vader on the Death Star. Not just appear, but even sit down and have entire conversations with his onetime apprentice.

Yoda and Anakin also appeared to Luke at the end of Return of the Jedi, smiling approvingly at Luke for completing their life's work. As far as we knew, these interactions with Luke would continue indefinitely since their guidance would probably be needed during Luke's efforts to rebuild the Jedi Order.

But if that's the case, then where were they while Snoke came to power? We're talking about a guy who literally picked up where the Emperor left off, subverted Kylo Ren, remade the Empire, and built a Mega Death Star that harnessed the power of an entire sun. Wouldn't that be the kind of thing the Jedi would want to get in front of?

To be fair, they only ever appeared to Luke, and we didn't even see him until the very end of the movie. So it's possible that they HAVE been appearing and we just haven't seen them because we haven't seen Luke. But even still, Anakin's other descendants could have used some guidance, especially the one that actually turned to the Dark Side.

I mean, Kylo Ren was begging Vader to send him a

message to guide him, yet Anakin still didn't appear to try and steer his grandson away from the edge of the cliff. Sure, it could have been because Kylo Ren wanted to go Dark Side, but Anakin more than anybody would have probably been able to talk some sense into him before things got out of hand.

Jar Jar Binks

Yeah, I know, he's probably the last guy most real Star Wars fans would ever want to see again, but as I talked about at great length in **The Unsolved Mysteries Of Star Wars**, despite surviving the fall of the Jedi, Jar Jar was MIA during the events of the original trilogy.

I've speculated a lot as to what became of the chronically useless Gungan after the rise of the Empire. I half expected him to pop up in Episode VII, and I'm not ruling out the possibility that he might make at least a quick appearance in one of the upcoming films.

The continuing mystery surrounding his fate leaves some interesting possibilities. I covered most of the good ones in the first book, but those aside, wouldn't it be gratifying to see him show up just long enough for Kylo Ren to ginsu him for the longtime fans who have made him a pariah?

Emperor Palpatine

You don't see this brought up very often, but if dead Jedi can appear to people in spectral form, wouldn't it stand to reason that Sith could do the same? We never had an occasion to find out since Return of the Jedi ended all of fifteen minutes after Vader and the Emperor did, but if we were going to see it, wouldn't now be the time?

It's possible that not just any Jedi or Sith can appear to the living, and since we haven't seen any dead Sith showing up in the previous movies, it's possible that this is just not something the Sith have in their repertoire. But if there was ever one Sith who had the power to cross that threshold, it would be Palpatine.

Once again, the caveat has to be that, if Palpatine was going to appear as a spirit, it wouldn't be to anyone we spent much time with during the movie. Most likely, he would only be appearing to Snoke, and since Snoke only appeared as a hologram to Kylo Ren and General Hux, we wouldn't know if he's in contact with the spirit of Palpatine when not Skyping with his underlings.

Boba Fett

Nobody reading this would be alone if they suspected that Boba Fett didn't truly meet his demise in the Sarlacc Pit. We're talking about the coolest, deadliest bounty hunter in movie history, and it just seems really anticlimactic for him to buy the farm that easily.

Plus, let's be real for a minute: Star Wars is a merchandising machine. If they found a way to bring Boba Fett back, think about how much they could cash in on all the new Boba Fett merchandise they could crank out.

This is all speculation, of course, since as far as we know, Boba Fett was indeed eaten by the Sarlacc Pit. But if it turned out he wasn't, wouldn't now be the perfect time for him to show up and come after Luke Skywalker for almost doing him in?

Is Qui-Gon Jinn A Grey Jedi?

*This feature originally appeared in **Darth Jar Jar (And Other Surprisingly Plausible Star Wars Theories)**, available now on Amazon Kindle and coming soon to paperback!*

Even though he took the lead role in Episode I, we didn't really get to know Qui-Gon Jinn all that well before he was killed by Darth Maul. What we do know is that he was a seasoned, veteran Jedi who was trusted enough to be put in charge of sensitive operations like the negotiations with the Trade Federation, but was still enough of a maverick that his tendency to follow his own path kept him from earning a seat on the Jedi High Council.

Even though he was obviously not a Sith or a malicious person by nature, it's pretty clear that his personal philosophies often fell outside the teachings of the Jedi Code. Despite his membership in the Jedi Order, his persona seems a bit more in line with that of a Grey Jedi rather than a traditional Jedi Knight.

For those who are unfamiliar with this special breed, the Grey Jedi were Force users who weren't out for galactic conquest like the Sith or personal gain like the Dark Jedi, but still disagreed enough with official Jedi teachings that it became difficult, or even impossible, for them to associate with the Jedi Order. They tended to follow their own way and refused to be constrained by the strictness of the Jedi Code, a description that certainly described Qui-Gon.

Another interesting thing about the Grey Jedi is that, even if they didn't take advantage of it, they were said to be capable of using both Light and Dark Side abilities. Even though we never saw Qui-Gon use Sith lightning or any other Dark Side abilities, the signs that he was not only able, but possibly even willing to do so were there.

Let's start with the most obvious: before he attained the rank of Jedi Knight, he was the Padawan to Count Dooku, who had turned to the Dark Side and become a Sith Lord by the time we met him in Episode II. Even before he turned, Dooku was known to be a political idealist and a man who was prone to following his heart and acting according to his own sense of right and wrong, whether or not it fell in line with the Jedi Code.

In fact, it's debatable whether or not Count Dooku can even reliably be called a true Sith Lord since he may have fallen more in line with the Grey Jedi philosophy depending on how you look at it. Dooku had already left the Jedi Order over the way he felt about the course the Republic had taken, and if he saw joining the Sith as the best way of pushing his political agenda, then he may not have been any more loyal to their core cause than he had been to that of the Jedi.

That willingness to walk the line between light and dark, not to mention the propensity to question the validity of any code of values being thrust upon him, would have been instilled in Qui-Gon very early in his days as a Padawan, and would have been carried into his life as a full-fledged Jedi Knight. Count Dooku seemed pretty convinced that Qui-Gon would have seen things his way if he hadn't died, and he may have been right given what we actually observed Qui-Gon saying shortly before his death.

When he discovered Anakin Skywalker on Tatooine and realized how high his Midichlorian count was, he decided on the spot that he was undoubtedly the Chosen One who would one day bring balance to the Force. He came to this conclusion without any input from the Council or any other Jedi, and assumed it was a foregone conclusion that Anakin's training would be approved before he even walked into the Council chamber.

Qui-Gon was so stunned when the Council rejected

Anakin that he said he would personally take Anakin on as a Padawan and see to his training from the ground up. The Council forbade him to do that since he already had a Padawan, and after arguing with the Council over Obi-Wan's eligibility to take the trials, decided he would outrightly defy the Jedi High Council and train Anakin anyway.

While Anakin was eventually accepted into the Jedi Order, Qui-Gon was killed before he had the chance to train the boy himself. It's interesting to think about how being trained by Qui-Gon instead of Obi-Wan might have affected Anakin in the long run, and if it could have led to him being even more bullheaded and defiant than he already was. Qui-Gon's own path was equally unclear, and it's possible that his continued friction with the Jedi Council could indeed have led to him following his own master's path out of the Jedi Order and into an ideal-driven existence.

Did Mace Windu Think He Was The Chosen One?

*The following feature originally appeared in **Darth Jar Jar (And Other Surprisingly Plausible Star Wars Theories)**, available now in the Kindle Store and coming soon to paperback!*

In spite of the fact that he was supposed to be one of the main good guys in the prequel trilogy, Mace Windu had this habit of coming off, to put it bluntly, like a real dick. While much of it can be explained away as him trying to project the image of a hard-as-steel leader, he definitely wasn't the most polished guy when it came to people skills, and one of the people he seemed to grate on the most was Anakin Skywalker.

The feeling was obviously mutual, because the fact that Mace never liked or trusted Anakin from the beginning came through as clear as day. He seemed unconvinced when Qui-Gon brought Anakin before the Jedi High Council to recommend him for training, and he had an almost disgusted look on his face when he broke the news to Qui-Gon that the boy wouldn't be trained after all.

Windu and Anakin definitely didn't get off on the right foot, and the Jedi Master didn't lighten up on Anakin one bit as the years passed. He outrightly told Obi-Wan that he didn't trust his apprentice, and questioned whether he was ready for the assignments he was being given. When Palpatine had Anakin appointed to the Jedi Council, Windu refused him the rank of Jedi Master and derisively told him to take a seat as if Anakin were somehow at fault for the arrangement.

You would think that after all that, Anakin might have finally scored some points when he came to Mace Windu to report that Palpatine was the Sith Lord they had been hunting for all those years. He didn't, because Mace made him wait in the Jedi Council chamber while he brought a team of Jedi to arrest the Chancellor himself.

It seems odd that someone in Mace Windu's position would treat the Chosen One so badly, and with hindsight being 20/20, you can see how his conduct became one of the key forces that pushed Anakin to the Dark Side. Mace Windu was the #2 Jedi in the Order behind Yoda, and also its #1 warrior, so why would he always come down so hard on the guy who was supposed to one day bring balance to the Force?

Could it be that Windu doubted Anakin because he believed himself to be the Chosen One? Is it possible that he thought he would be the one to bring balance to the Force, and that's why he resented Anakin, whom he regarded as an undisciplined pretender? Everyone else seemed to take it as a given that Anakin was the guy, but the evidence was there that Windu not only felt threatened by Anakin, but jealously held him back from his destiny to try and steal it for himself.

Why would Mace Windu have such a profoundly overinflated self-image? Let's start with the obvious: he's an incredibly powerful fighter, the best in the Jedi Order, and one of the best in the history of that organization. Part of that power was derived from his rare and complex Force ability to see shatterpoints, faultlines in people and events that could be exploited through use of the Force to achieve a desired end.

This was a very useful ability in combat, as Windu could see an opponent's weak points and pour the Force into them to tear them down from the inside out. He also had the ability to use the talent outside of combat, finding shatterpoints in his surroundings that could be manipulated to make events play out in one way or another.

Mace Windu also created his own form of lightsaber combat that actually drew on the Dark Side to grant him additional power in battle. No other Jedi risked using this form because Windu was the only Jedi who was ever able to use it without turning himself, and he no doubt felt that his ability to balance both sides of the Force in such a way made him special.

Then there was the fact that he was, of course, the second highest-ranking member of the Jedi Order, and one day would be #1 when Yoda died or retired or whatever. How could anyone BUT the top Jedi be the Chosen One, the man with the right stuff who could wipe out the Sith once and for all?

The more you examine the situation, the more likely it seems that Mace Windu felt like Anakin Skywalker was stealing his thunder. It apparently didn't matter to him if the Jedi weren't supposed to be prideful or arrogant (qualities he derided in Anakin, by the way), he didn't spend his entire life working to attain everything he had so some hick from a two-bit planet outside the Republic could show up one day, leapfrog him, and become the hero of the entire galaxy.

Even though he may have convinced himself that he had good reasons for doing so, Mace Windu started cutting Anakin's legs out from under him every chance he got. Palpatine's comment to Anakin that the Jedi didn't trust him and weren't treating him fairly might have carried a lot less weight if Mace Windu hadn't shut him out the way he had.

This literally continued up to the very moment Windu got himself killed. Despite the fact that the Chosen One from the prophecy was standing right next to him, Windu defied the devoutly-held teachings when he tried to take it upon himself to kill the Emperor. Anakin was right: killing an enemy in cold blood wasn't the honorable thing to do, and he knew because he had just done it himself to Count Dooku, and he was convinced that the Jedi couldn't act legitimately without arresting and trying him.

For his part, Anakin respected Mace Windu and

desperately wanted his approval, but Windu never gave it simply because he didn't WANT to believe that Anakin was the Chosen One. Anakin's faith in the Jedi had been badly, badly shaken by that point, and this appeal to Mace Windu was literally his last ditch effort to salvage his own faith in the Order he had spent his entire adult life in service to.

It literally fell on deaf ears because Mace Windu was so focused on destroying the Sith and doing it himself that he didn't even seem to hear Anakin. Anakin did have a personal interest in keeping the Emperor alive, but nothing he said about the ethics involved in what Windu was about to do was wrong.

Windu swung the lightsaber down, was dead thirty seconds later, and had nobody to blame but himself. He could have done the right thing for the Jedi by standing aside and giving the Chosen One the latitude to do what he needed to, but he did what was right for Mace Windu instead and put the boot down on him every chance he got. His selfish need to be a hero led to the destruction of the Jedi, and handed the galaxy right over to the Sith.

About The Author

As you've probably guessed by now, I am Stuart Carapola: the mind behind StarWarsWavelength.com, writer, entertainer, and lifelong Star Wars geek from upstate New York. This is not a picture of me. It is, however, what I found when I went on Google and typed my first name and "glamour shot". Try it, everyone I know comes up with something really bizarre when they do that. If you want to see what I really look like, you can find me on Facebook at www.facebook.com/whereitsat42, or on Twitter at @StuartCarapola! If you do, I promise I'll post lots of really cool stuff about upcoming books, sales on my existing titles, and whatever else spills out of my mind at any given moment!

16260666R00068

Printed in Poland
by Amazon Fulfillment
Poland Sp. z o.o., Wrocław